engage

We dare you not to be amazed
We'll look at Revelation — the
Bible; Matthew talks us through some of Jesus' most
challenging teaching; we'll also ask big questions about
sin, sanctification and body art.

✱ DAILY READINGS Each day's
page throws you into the Bible, to
get you handling, questioning and
exploring God's message to you —
encouraging you to act on it and talk
to God more in prayer.

THIS ISSUE: Read a biography of
Jesus in **Matthew;** have your mind
blown by **Revelation;** watch a royal
soap opera in **2 Samuel;** and catch
rarely heard words in **Obadiah.**

✱ ESSENTIAL Articles on the
basics we really need to know about
God, the Bible and Christianity. This
issue, we look at what the Bible says
about **sanctification.**

✱ TAKE IT FURTHER If you're
hungry for more at the end of an
engage page, turn to the **Take it
further** section to dig deeper.

✱ STUFF Articles on stuff relevant
to the lives of young Christians. This
issue: **tattoos and piercings.**

✱ REAL LIVES True stories,
revealing God at work in people's
lives. This time — **we go to France
to meet Kevin Mosi Da Costa.**

✱ TOOLBOX is full of tools
to help you understand the Bible.
This issue we concentrate on
the Bible's big story.

✱ TRICKY tackles those mind-
bendingly tricky questions that
confuse us all, as well as questions
our friends bombard us with.
This time we ask: **Why do I keep
sinning?**

All of us who work on **engage** are
passionate to see the Bible at
work in people's lives. Do you
want God's word to have an
impact on your life? Then open
your Bible, and start on the first
engage study right now...

HOW TO USE engage

1 Set a time you can read the Bible every day

2 Find a place where you can be quiet and think

3 Grab your Bible, pen and a notebook

4 Ask God to help you understand what you read

5 Read the day's verses with engage, taking time to think about it

6 Pray about what you've read

BIBLE STUFF We use the NIV Bible version, so you might find it's the best one to use with engage. If the notes say **"Read Matthew 1 v 1–17"**, look up Matthew in the contents page at the front of your Bible. It'll tell you which page Matthew starts on. Find chapter 1 of Matthew, and then verse 1 of chapter 1 (the verse numbers are the tiny ones). Then start reading. Simple.

In this issue...

ENGAGE 13 IS BROUGHT TO YOU BY...

Writers: Martin "Beardy" Cole   Cassie "No tattoos" Martin
        Helen "Sanctified" Thorne

Designer: Steve "Stairway to heaven" Devane

Proof-readers Anne "Grammar guardian" Woodcock   Nicole "Eagle eyes" Carter

Editor: Martin "Two nicknames" Cole (martin@thegoodbook.co.uk)

Matthew

The big picture

Ever read a biography? Maybe a sporting one or celebrity memoirs? You get to see how the big-name star in question started out. Perhaps with some embarrassing baby photos and the awkward teenage years with a bad haircut and goofy teeth, before they hit the big time and become impossibly glamorous.

Well, the book of Matthew is one of the four Gospels — biographies of Jesus — and seems to have been written for a largely Jewish audience. No amusing childhood pranks or Oscar wins here though. The opening verses of chapter one give us a big clue about what's important to Matthew as he writes. In verse one he points out that Jesus is descended from Abraham and David. In short, Jesus is heir to the promises of the Old Testament and heir to a throne.

Matthew wants to show how Jesus Christ came as the completion of Old Testament teaching and prophecy (words from God about the future).

Matthew has 53 direct Old T quotes and loads more passing references. He's showing us how Jesus fits into the big picture of God's word.

Matthew uses the Old Testament to prove that Jesus is the long-awaited Messiah — the King God promised He would send to rescue His people — and the Saviour of the world. He'd come for all people, not just Jews. The news of this big rescue was now for everyone.

Matthew wants his readers (and that includes us) to realise just how significant Jesus' arrival on this planet was. The promised one, the perfect Son of God, the King of the universe is here. Will you bow the knee to Him now or be forced to when He returns in glory? Will you take this biography to heart?

1 | Family album

Does your heart sink when you see a long list of names in the Bible? Well this one is full of hidden treasures and surprises — it's also a neat summary of God's dealings with His people from the Old Testament 'til Jesus' birth.

👁 Read Matthew 1 v 1–17

ENGAGE YOUR BRAIN

▶ *What words or phrases are used in v1 to describe who Jesus is?*

The Messiah or Christ was the king promised in the Old Testament who would lead God's people. In fact, prophets such as Isaiah claimed this king would be God Himself! So why are David and Abraham mentioned? Take a look at the promises God made to both of them. This descendant, Jesus, was about to make God's promises come true!

▶ *What did God promise to Abraham in Genesis 12 v 1–3?*

▶ *And to David in 2 Samuel 7 v 12–16?*

A few names are worth mentioning — Abraham was a big hero, but his grandson Jacob was a bit of a mixed bag. Perez had a tough start in life. Rahab and Ruth weren't even Israelites; they were hated outsiders. King Ahaz was evil, but Hezekiah had his heart in the right place.

▶ *What does this tell us about who God uses in His plans?*

▶ *What does this tell us about God?*

Matthew picks up on some major landmarks in Jewish history as he gives us a snapshot overview not only of Jesus' human origins but of God's dealings with His people over hundreds of years.

PRAY ABOUT IT

Thank God that He uses ordinary people to bring His plan of rescue to the world. Thank Him that He keeps His promises. Thank Him that He chose you despite your sin. Ask Him to help you learn more about Jesus — the Christ — as you read through Matthew.

→ TAKE IT FURTHER

Get the picture on page 109.

2 ¦ What's in a name?

We've seen Jesus' family tree; now Matthew gives us a close-up as we zoom in to focus on His birth.

👁 Read Matthew 1 v 18–25

ENGAGE YOUR BRAIN

▶ What was unusual about Jesus' conception? (v18, 25)

▶ Why is this so important?

Jesus had a human mother and so was fully human but was also fully God — note the references to Him being conceived from the Holy Spirit. This makes Him uniquely qualified for His mission — more about which we'll discover later.

▶ What would Joseph have assumed had happened?

▶ Why is Joseph described as righteous? What could he have done instead? (v19)

▶ How does God reassure him? (v20)

▶ What's the baby to be called?

▶ What other name will Jesus be known by, according to Isaiah's prophesy? (v23)?

▶ What two crucial things do these names tell us about the reason Jesus was born into our world?

A miraculous conception. God in human flesh entering our world — Immanuel, God is with us. And God with a mission — to save sinners.

PRAY ABOUT IT

God becoming human — is one of the most incredible things to ever happen. The other is that He came to die for sinners like you and me. Take some time to really let that sink in and thank God for His incredible rescue plan.

THE BOTTOM LINE

Jesus is God with us.

→ TAKE IT FURTHER

Find a little more on page 109.

5

3 | We two kings?

Another well known part of the Christmas story today — or is it? No mention of camels and we aren't told how many Magi or wise men there were. But this is a story about kings: two to be precise.

👁 Read Matthew 2 v 1–12

ENGAGE YOUR BRAIN

▶ *Who are the two kings mentioned? (v1–2)*

▶ *What do we learn about Jesus?*
v2:
v6:
v11:

▶ *And Herod?*
v7–8:
v12:

▶ *Why do you think Herod was frightened by the thought of a new king?*

▶ *How did the wise men respond to the news of this king? (v10-11)*

Jesus still has this effect today. At one level Herod was right to see a threat to his kingship. Jesus is THE King and we can't call the shots if He takes His rightful place as ruler of our lives. But the Magi had a better reaction — they recognised Jesus' kingship and took great time and trouble to come and bow before Him, offering Him costly presents.

GET ON WITH IT

Have you recognised Jesus' right to rule over your life? The Magi travelled a long way at great personal cost to see Jesus. Is that attitude part of your Christian life? Do you spend time with Jesus even when you'd rather stay in bed than read your Bible? Do you make the effort to go to church or youth group even if other plans seem more tempting?

PRAY ABOUT IT

The Magi weren't even Jews and yet they came to recognise Jesus as their King. Thank God that Jesus came for the whole world and pray for the parts of it where people still don't know the true King.

THE BOTTOM LINE

There can only be one King in your life. Make sure it's Jesus.

→ TAKE IT FURTHER

What did Micah say? Page 109.

4 | Murder in mind

Herod was a puppet king, put in place by the Romans. Paranoid and dangerous, he had anyone he saw as competition murdered; even his own wife and sons. Now he's set his sights on Jesus. What's going to happen?

👁 Read Matthew 2 v 13–23

ENGAGE YOUR BRAIN
▷ *What are Herod's intentions? (v13)*
▷ *What does he do? (v16)*
▷ *How is Jesus protected? (v13–15)*

Even this horrific slaughter was foretold by the prophets (v18), as is Jesus' escape (v15) and even His childhood hometown (v23). There are no coincidences or mistakes here. God had a plan from the beginning of time.

▷ *What title was Jesus given back in v2?*
▷ *When is he called that again? (Hint: chapter 27 v 37)*

Jesus faced hostility, hatred and murderous violence almost from birth. His Father kept Him safe from Herod but only for a while — it was not yet time for Jesus to die. He didn't save Him at Golgotha but turned His face away. Why? Remember why Jesus came? To save sinners.

PRAY ABOUT IT
Amazingly God turned people's sinful, hate-filled rejection of the King into the very means by which they could be rescued. Thank Him now.

SHARE IT
Your non-Christian friends and family probably don't come across like Herod. But rejecting Jesus is as serious and as ugly as what Herod did. Rejecting our King is treason and deserves the death penalty. Herod died (v19) and so will we. Only by accepting Jesus' death in our place can we live at peace under His rule in His kingdom forever. Can you share that great news with someone today?

THE BOTTOM LINE
Rejecting the King is treason.

→ TAKE IT FURTHER
Justice and mercy on page 109.

5 Make way for the King

Time has moved on. Jesus has grown up now and just as a King has a herald announcing his arrival, here we see John the Baptist doing exactly that.

Read Matthew 3 v 1–12

ENGAGE YOUR BRAIN

▶ What is John's message? (v2)

Repenting means turning away from our sins and turning back to God. The kingdom of heaven is near because the King is near!

▶ Who does Isaiah say John is? (v3)

▶ So who is coming? (v3)

Some theologians have called John the Baptist the last Old Testament prophet. He is pointing to the coming King, the Messiah. As Isaiah's prophecy makes clear, John's call means that the Lord, God Himself, is on His way. Cue Jesus!

▶ What warning does John have for those who show no evidence of repentance? (v7–10)

▶ What does John tell us about the coming King? (v11–12)

Jesus came to bring judgment (v12). We know that when He returns He will judge the earth, but that process began when He came the first time. People's reactions to Jesus — as we will see over the course of Matthew's Gospel — would either save them or condemn them.

GET ON WITH IT

The Pharisees and Sadducees thought they were OK because they were descended from Abraham, but they faced Jesus' judgment. Do you think you're OK because you go to church, or your parents are Christians or you're a nice person? Repent! Turn to the King — He alone can save you.

THE BOTTOM LINE

The King is coming! Get ready!

→ TAKE IT FURTHER

More background stuff on page 110.

6 | Making a big splash

The King arrives. Jesus is now 30. The next big
event confirms who He is. It's surprisingly soggy.

Read Matthew 3 v 13–17

ENGAGE YOUR BRAIN

▶ Why has Jesus come to the Jordan? (v13)

▶ Why does John not want to baptise Jesus? (v14)

▶ Why does Jesus say John should baptise Him? (v15)

You can understand John's hesitation — here's the person he's just been talking about, someone massively above him, the King Himself, and He's asking to be baptised? John's baptism is for repentant sinners, not the perfect Messiah!

But what sort of a Messiah is Jesus? What sort of King is He? He's not up there with John telling sinners to repent, although He does preach that message later. No, He's down there in the water with the sinners; showing He's one of them even though He has no need of cleansing.

▶ What is God the Father's verdict on Jesus? (v16–17)

▶ Bearing in mind Jesus' actions here and His Father's words, why is the cross such an extraordinary, amazing happening?

PRAY ABOUT IT

"God made him who had no sin to be sin for us, so that in him we might become the righteousness of God." (2 Corinthians 5 v 21)

Think about what this meant for Jesus, and what it means for you, and then talk to God about it.

THE BOTTOM LINE

Jesus came for sinners.

➔ TAKE IT FURTHER

More exciting explanation on p110.

9

7 Temptation situation

The heavens opened and God spoke, confirming who Jesus was. Here, on earth, was His Son, the unique God-man. Now... would Jesus live up to that and complete His task? Or not trust God and disobey Him, like the rest of us?

👁 **Read Matthew 4 v 1–11**

Answer the following questions:

	Israel	Jesus
How long were they tested?	Numbers 32 v 13	Matthew 4 v 2
How do they respond to lack of food?	Exodus 16 v 1–3	v3–4
Do they put God to the test?	Exodus 17 v 1–2	v5–7
Do they worship God alone?	Exodus 32 v 1-6	v8–10

God's people failed to live His way again and again. They couldn't overcome their sin, but with Jesus' arrival we see a new Israel: a Jew who is totally obedient to God, someone who fulfils all the promises of the Old Testament. This is the start of something exciting.

PRAY ABOUT IT

Thank God that Jesus is the one perfect human being. Say sorry for the times you fail to trust God, grumble and put other things before serving Him. Thank Him that Jesus was not only totally obedient but that His obedience led Him to die so that you could be forgiven.

➔ TAKE IT FURTHER

Jesus v the devil: further coverage on page 110.

8 ¦ Light and life ¦

The preparation is over. Now this unique God-man can begin His public ministry. Again we see Jesus living up to prophecies made many hundreds of years before. God's plans are made reality.

👁 Read Matthew 4 v 12

ENGAGE YOUR BRAIN

▷ *What has happened to John?*

Read Matthew 14 v 1–12 for the distressing outcome.

👁 Read Matthew 4 v 13–17

▷ *Are you prepared to face the consequences of living God's way, no matter how serious?*

▷ *What does Isaiah say about Jesus? (v16)*

▷ *What does Jesus say people need to do to enter his kingdom? (v17)*

Repenting doesn't just mean feeling sorry for the things we've done wrong — most people feel like that at some point. No, it's an active decision to turn away from one way of living and to turn back to God. Remember how John the Baptist preached the same message? But this time, the King is calling us to repent! It's His kingdom of light and life which is near. Get out of the darkness!

PRAY ABOUT IT

Have you done that? Pray for people you know who are living in darkness, that they would see Jesus' light and turn to Him.

THE BOTTOM LINE

Jesus is light and life.

→ TAKE IT FURTHER

Step into the light of page 110.

9 | Something fishy

The kingdom is near and things are starting to gather momentum. Here we see Jesus calling the first disciples.

👁 Read Matthew 4 v 18–22

ENGAGE YOUR BRAIN

▶ *Who does Jesus see? (v18)*

▶ *What does He say to them? (v19)*

▶ *What do they do? (v20)*

▶ *How about verses 21-22?*

▶ *What is so surprising about their responses?*

Jesus is the King. When a King tells you to do something, you do it. Peter, Andrew, James and John don't fully realise who Jesus is yet, but they recognise something of His authority.

▶ *Are you following the King?*

▶ *What do you think Jesus means by "fish for people" / "fishers of men"?*

Being a fisherman wasn't a glamorous job. Antisocial hours, hard work, often with little success, and smelling fishy. Nice. We might not have to deal with the personal hygiene part but fishing for people will often be similar — hard work, often with limited "success", but remember v16. We have a wonderful and life-saving message to share.

👁 Read verses 23–25

...and remind yourself what a powerful and compassionate King Jesus is.

PRAY ABOUT IT

Ask for God's help to fish for people.

GET ON WITH IT

As you head out into whatever you face this week — school, college, work, home — leave a mental "gone fishing" sign on your bedroom door.

→ TAKE IT FURTHER

Go fishing on page 110.

10 | Blessed is best

Here are the beatitudes: Jesus' teaching on what it means to be "blessed", on what sort of a life is worth having. What sort of life do you want? Think for a minute...

Read Matthew 5 v 1–5

ENGAGE YOUR BRAIN

- *What sort of person do you think God would want in heaven?*
- *Do verses 3–12 sound like that?*
- *How would you define "blessed"?*
- *What might it mean to be "poor in spirit"?*
- *Why is this necessary to enter the kingdom of heaven?*

"Poor in spirit" could be rephrased as "spiritually bankrupt" — our state when we realise we have nothing to offer God. Ironically, the entrance requirement for God's kingdom is not top grades, a great CV/resume, or hundreds of good works for charity, but recognising that you have nothing to offer. You can't receive a gift unless your hands are empty first.

- *How does the second beatitude follow on from the first? (v4)*
- *How do you think those who mourn will be comforted?*
- *What is meekness and how does it follow on from the previous two attitudes?*

Why do we have nothing to offer God? It's not just that we're not good enough. We're also really bad. We are sinners who reject our loving Creator. That's something we should mourn. Once we have the right view about ourselves, we will be meek not arrogant, humble not proud, and amazingly that is when we are blessed and God approves of us, because of Jesus.

PRAY ABOUT IT

Think about verses 3–5. Have you gone through that process? Realising you have nothing to offer God, mourning your sin, humbling yourself before Him? Spend some time praying through those verses now.

THE BOTTOM LINE

Blessed are the poor in spirit.

TAKE IT FURTHER

Count your blessings on page 110.

13

11

Count your blessings

This list of "blessed are the..." is known as the beatitudes, and sometimes called beautiful attitudes. As we saw from verses 3–5, they build up a picture of what it looks like to be part of the kingdom of heaven.

👁 Read Matthew 5 v 6–12

ENGAGE YOUR BRAIN

▶ *Try to define each of these six beatitudes in your own words.*
v6:

v7:

v8:

v9:

v10:

v11–12:

THINK IT OVER

Do you really hunger and thirst for righteousness? Do you long for the day when Jesus will return and your sin will vanish forever?

GET ON WITH IT

Do you ever think about that part of the Lord's Prayer that says *"forgive us our sins as we forgive those who sin against us"* and feel a bit guilty?

Jesus tells us that His followers should be merciful to others for they have received and will receive God's mercy. Are you holding a grudge against anyone? Need to forgive someone even if they haven't said sorry? Do it.

▶ *Why might being a peacemaker (v9) show a family resemblance to God?*

▶ *What does Jesus warn us about in verses 10–11?*

▶ *How does he encourage us?*

PRAY ABOUT IT

Thank God that when Jesus died on the cross, He washed our sinful hearts clean so that one day we will see Him face to face.

THE BOTTOM LINE

Blessed are the pure in heart for they will see God.

➡ TAKE IT FURTHER

Walk on the path of peace to p111.

12 | A salt course

Have you ever been called "salt of the earth"? Unlikely — it conjures up visions of a weather-beaten old farmer chewing straw and dispensing sage advice to youngsters. But salt of the earth is what Jesus calls members of His kingdom, regardless of their age or background.

👁 **Read Matthew 5 v 13–16**

ENGAGE YOUR BRAIN

▶ How do you think living out the beatitudes makes Christians salt and light in our world?

▶ What function does salt have — it must be good for something? (see v13)

Various ideas have been suggested for what Jesus means in verse 13. Salt is a preservative — it stops food rotting, so Christians must be there to slow the decay of society's morals. Salt is antiseptic — it stops germs — same idea again. Salt adds flavour; salt was very valuable in ancient times. Whatever Jesus means by using this metaphor, it's clear that Christians should be having a positive effect on the world around us.

▶ What purpose does a light serve? (v15)

▶ How are we to be lights? (v16)

▶ How have these verses challenged you personally?

PRAY ABOUT IT

Ask God to help you have a positive impact on the world around you and that as people see your good deeds they would give glory to our Father in heaven.

GET ON WITH IT

Is there an issue in the news, or locally or at school/college/work where you could make a positive contribution as a Christian? How can you glorify God in the way you get involved?

THE BOTTOM LINE

Jesus says: "YOU are the salt of the earth".

➔ **TAKE IT FURTHER**

Light-hearted stuff on page 111.

Tattoos and piercings

Tattoos are no longer just for hairy bikers who want "I love mum" tattooed on their arms. Celebs have them, your friends may have them, but should Christians have them? And what about piercings? We don't seem to fuss about pierced ears, so why not eyebrows, tongues or bellybuttons?

You might be reading this thinking: "Why not? It's just your outward appearance, it doesn't make any difference to what you believe." But then again, you might have heard Christian leaders saying: "Absolutely no way!" or even calling it a sin.

The main verse people use against tattoos is Leviticus 19 v 28: *"Do not cut your bodies for the dead or put tattoo marks on yourselves. I am the LORD."* Seems pretty clear, but this passage and the surrounding bits are specifically dealing with the religious rituals of the people living around the Israelites. God's desire is to set His people apart from other cultures, and He knows idol worship will lead them away from the one true God.

In the Leviticus passage, v26 tells us: *"Do not eat any meat with the blood still in it"* and v27: *"Do not cut the hair at the sides of your head or clip off the edges of your beard."* Back then these customs were associated with pagan rites and rituals. But getting a haircut is not a sign of anything much these days and the New Testament has clearly told us that eating non-kosher food is fine (Acts 10 v 9–15). So, is getting a tattoo a form of pagan worship that's still forbidden by God today?

Likewise, ear-piercing in the Old Testament was a sign of slavery — in fact when God rescued the Israelites from slavery in Egypt, they were told to remove their earrings as a sign that they'd been redeemed. But now, ear piercing doesn't carry that particular symbolism any more, so surely it's OK? It seems fair to say that these are what the Bible calls disputable matters (see Romans 14).

The right question isn't "Is it okay for a Christian to have a tattoo or piercing?" but "Is it OK for me in my situation to have a tattoo/piercing?"

The New Testament doesn't address the rights or wrongs of ear-piercing directly but it does say: *"Your beauty should not come from outward adornment, such as braided hair and the wearing of gold jewellery and fine clothes. Instead, it should be that of your inner self, the unfading beauty of a gentle and quiet spirit, which is of great worth in God's sight."* (1 Peter 3 v 3–4).

So perhaps rather than saying: "Yes, tattoos and piercings are fine" or "No, Christians definitely shouldn't have them", we should ask ourselves the following questions:

- *What are my motives for wanting a tattoo/piercing? Our bodies are God's, not our own (1 Corinthians 6 v 19–20); am I seeking to glorify God or draw attention to myself?*

- *Am I conforming to the world or am I more interested in becoming like Christ? (Romans 12 v 1–2) Am I fitting in when I should be standing out?*

- *What specific image or words do I have in mind? Even if you're persuaded that having a tattoo is acceptable, the specific design might send the wrong message.*

- *Will getting a tattoo or piercing cause me to disobey my parents? As Christians we're called to honour our parents and that means respecting their wishes.*

It's also worth remembering that tattoos are painful to have done, pretty much permanent (and even more painful and expensive to remove), and carry some health risks. Likewise piercings are not risk-free and can cause medical complications in certain parts of the body.

But the best words to finish with are from 1 Corinthians 10 v 23–24: "'I have the right to do anything,' you say — but not everything is beneficial. 'I have the right to do anything' — but not everything is constructive. No one should seek their own good, but the good of others."

What's in it for God?

Revelation

Revealing Jesus

Beasts with seven heads. Angels sending plagues. Horses with snakes' tails. The moon turned blood red. The number 666. Armageddon. Dragons. Welcome to Revelation.

Are you excited about reading it? Or worried? Relax. To understand Revelation, all you need is God's help and your Bible. *Engage* will simply show you how the Old Testament helps us unwrap Revelation — all the weird, noisy, fiery, surreal bits too.

Above all, this book is a revelation of Jesus. It teaches us that Jesus has already won the great battle over everything that opposes God and His people. Amazingly, dying on the cross was Jesus' decisive victory. And because Jesus has won, His task when He returns is to get rid of His enemies once and for all.

Before that time, Revelation warns that life will most likely be rough, painful and puzzling. Particularly for Christians. But Jesus has won. So stick with Him and hang in there.

Revelation is full of pictures, symbols and numbers. Take them literally and you're in for a nightmare. But the rest of the Bible helps us understand many of them. The most used numbers in revelation are these:

3 = repetition for emphasis
4 = the whole of creation
6 = the human number
7 = completion/perfection
12 = God's true people

We'll explain *why* they're understood like this as we go along. Other numbers and many symbols are mentioned, and we'll explain them too!

13 ¦ Let's get started ¦

Revelation is a letter written by John, the disciple of Jesus, about a vision God gave him. It's also a prophecy — teaching us about the future, as well as the past and the present. Most of all it's a revelation of who Jesus is.

👁 **Read Revelation 1 v 1–3**

ENGAGE YOUR BRAIN

▶ How does John describe this book? (v1)

▶ What must we do to really benefit from Revelation? (v3)

Revelation contains loads of pictures, visions and weird stuff. But, ultimately, it's revealing Jesus to us. As He really is now. So read it, make sure you really hear what God's saying, and take it to heart.

👁 **Read verses 4–8**

▶ How is God the Father described? (v4, 8)

▶ How about Jesus? (v5)

▶ What has He done for us? (v5–6)

▶ What will happen when He returns? (v7)

The number seven appears immediately. In Revelation, seven stands for perfection and completeness. John sent this letter to seven churches — but it's for the whole church, all Christians. The "seven spirits" (v4) means the Holy Spirit, who is completely perfect.

Verses 5–6 vividly describe Jesus and His relationship with us. He faithfully witnessed to the truth and was killed. He was raised from death as the first of many God will raise (all believers, when Jesus returns!). He is now in heaven as the Ruler of everything.

PRAY ABOUT IT

Jesus loves us and died on the cross to free all believers from their sins. In fact, He's made them into a kingdom and priests who will live with and serve God for ever. Get thanking and praising Him right now!

→ **TAKE IT FURTHER**

The lowdown on Revelation — p111.

14 | Son shining

The Christian life is often tough. But however rough, God is in control. It's easy to forget that it's Jesus Christ who has ultimate authority in this world of ours.

👁 Read Revelation 1 v 9–11

ENGAGE YOUR BRAIN

▷ What were John and these Christians sharing in? (v9)

▷ What did the voice tell John to do? (v11)

John told people about Jesus and so was chased away and forced to live on the island of Patmos. He reminds us in v9 that the Christian life isn't easy; in this world we must stick together as we face suffering and tough times, waiting for Jesus' return.

👁 Read verses 12–16

▷ How is this incredible person described?

▷ Where was He standing and what was in His hands? (v13, 16)

The name "son of man" (v13) is from the book of Daniel, and describes someone who was given worldwide, eternal authority by God.

👁 Read verses 17–20

▷ How does this person describe Himself? (v18)

▷ What must John write? (v19)

▷ So what's Revelation about?

▷ What's the deal with the stars and the lampstands? (v20)

This is Jesus. Read through verses 12–18 again and see how He's not the weak, cuddly character many people see Him as, but the all-powerful ruler of the universe!

THINK IT OVER

At that time, Christians were in real danger of losing their lives for their faith. If ever we are, then what encouragement is there in this passage that we won't be losers?

PRAY ABOUT IT

The church may seem weak, but at its centre is the person with complete authority. For all eternity. Thank God for Jesus right now.

→ TAKE IT FURTHER

More mind-blowing stuff on p111.

15 | Church news letter

There are seven letters to seven churches. Since seven in Revelation is the complete number, these letters are to the whole church, all over the world. So what Jesus said to these churches, He's saying to you and your church.

👁 **Read Revelation 2 v 1–7**

ENGAGE YOUR BRAIN

▶ What good things does Jesus say about these Christians? (v2–3)

▶ What criticisms did He have? (v4)

▶ So what should they do? (v5)

▶ What's the threat? (v5)

▶ What's the reward? (v7)

These guys worked hard for the gospel and hung in there during hard times. They got rid of false teachers who were trying to drag them down. But they'd lost their first love — it seems their initial enthusiasm for Jesus and living His way had tailed off dramatically. They'd be in serious trouble unless they sorted this out. And what a great reward for those who love and serve Jesus — eternal life with Him (v7).

👁 **Read verses 8–11**

▶ What problems did the church in Smyrna have? (v9)

▶ How did Jesus encourage them? (v10)

▶ What's the great promise? (v11)

Jargon buster: "synagogue of Satan" = Jews who persecuted Christians; "ten days" = a limited time; "second death" = being punished at God's final judgment. Anyway, these guys were being terribly persecuted for their faith. BUT... they were truly rich for suffering for Jesus and would be given the crown of eternal life!

PRAY ABOUT IT

Have you lost your love for Jesus? What will you do about it? What will you say to Him and ask Him right now? Pray that you'll keep going through the dark times, looking forward to glorious eternity.

→ **TAKE IT FURTHER**

News extra on page 112.

16 ¦ Good news, bad news

In John's incredible vision, Jesus told him to write to seven churches. Let's see what Jesus said to churches 3 and 4. Remember, this message is for the whole church — that means all Christians.

👁 Read Revelation 2 v 12–17

ENGAGE YOUR BRAIN

- ▶ *How was Pergamum described? (v13)*
- ▶ *What was good about this church? (v13)*
- ▶ *What was not so good? (v14-15)*
- ▶ *What's the warning? (v16)*

Pergamum was a tough place to be a Christian. Roman emperors and gods were worshipped and Christians were persecuted or even killed (v13). So these believers were commended for not giving up on Jesus. However, they'd listened to false teachers and were involved in idol worship and sexual sin. Jesus told them to repent and turn back to Him.

👁 Read verse 18–29

- ▶ *What had these Christians got right? (v19)*
- ▶ *What was wrong here? (v20)*
- ▶ *What was the bad news for the woman who was leading them astray? (v21–23)*

The church in Thyatira was doing great things (v19); but some of them were involved in idol worship and sexual sin. A female prophet in the church was behind most of it and was rightly punished for it. Yet for those who kept obeying Jesus, they would share in His rule and authority. What an amazing promise — one day believers will rule with Jesus!

GET ON WITH IT

- ▶ *What do you "worship" more than God?*
- ▶ *How do you disobey God when it comes to sex stuff?*
- ▶ *What do you need to do about these things?*

PRAY ABOUT IT

Talk to God about this stuff and ask Him to help you overcome these sins.

→ TAKE IT FURTHER

Nicolaitans, hidden manna and the morning star... page 112.

17 | Poking and perking

We all need a poke in the ribs sometimes — that's what the Christians in Sardis receive here. We also need encouragement and a pat on the back too, just as the church in Philadelphia did.

Read Revelation 3 v 1–6

ENGAGE YOUR BRAIN

- What did people think of this church? What was the truth? (v1)

- What must they do? (v2)

- How? (v3)

- What if they didn't? (v3)

- What's the evidence that there were some who had a real relationship with Jesus? (v4)

- What's promised to them? (v4–5)

Read verse 7–13

- How does Jesus encourage this church? (v8–9)

- How else? (v10)

- So what should they do in the meantime? (v11)

- What do you think v12 means?

There were only a small number of Christians in Philadelphia, a city with many Jews who were saying: "You Christians aren't the true people of God. We are. It's us who belong in the temple and city of God, not you!" Life was tough for Christians there, and they were feeling weak. But God would protect them and one day they'd be strong (like pillars, v12) and would be with God for ever.

THINK IT OVER

- What would Jesus challenge you about?
- What would He urge you to change?
- How has He encouraged you through His words in Revelation?

PRAY ABOUT IT

Talk these issues over with God. And pray for any Christians you know who are in the minority and feeling weak.

→ TAKE IT FURTHER

Open the door to page 113.

18 | Lukewarm Laodicea

Laodicea was a wealthy city with loads of successful industries. The last of Jesus' seven letters was written to the Christians who lived there. And it was a huge wake-up call for them.

👁 Read Revelation 3 v 14

ENGAGE YOUR BRAIN
▶ *What do these descriptions of Jesus tell us about Him?*

"Amen" is the Hebrew word for "truth". Jesus is the truth and speaks the truth. He's totally faithful and we can trust everything He says. He rules all of God's creation. Listen to Him.

👁 Read verses 15–18
▶ *What was the problem? (v14–15)*

▶ *How did they view themselves? (v17)*

▶ *What didn't they realise? (v17)*

▶ *What must they do? (v18)*

These Christians were lukewarm — not having the guts to live for Jesus wholeheartedly. Laodicea was famous for its wealth, fabrics and eye ointment ("salve"). Jesus told them their wealth was worth nothing; they needed true riches from Jesus. They needed to cover their shamefulness. And to see they must turn away from selfish living and start obeying God.

👁 Read verses 19–22
▶ *What should these guys do? (v19)*

▶ *What's the great offer? (v20)*

▶ *What's the reward for those who accept Jesus' offer? (v21)*

Money and possessions may make us *feel* secure, but only trusting in Jesus can bring us eternal security.

PRAY ABOUT IT
Pray for friends (maybe yourself too) who rely on money and possessions but really need the security of life with Jesus.

THE BOTTOM LINE
True riches are only found in Jesus.

→ TAKE IT FURTHER
Feeling lukewarm? Try page 113.

19 | Heavenly view

The scene now switches from earth to heaven. John is given a front-row view right inside. Come and sit on his shoulders to see.

👁 **Read Revelation 4 v 1–6**

ENGAGE YOUR BRAIN

▶ *What does John see at the centre of heaven? (v2)*

▶ *What do you think v3–5 tells us about the person on the throne?*

Verses 3–6 are full of Old Testament references (eg: the rainbow recalls God's promise to Noah and His power shown in the flood). John's telling us exactly who's on the throne — it's the God of Noah, of Moses, the God who gave His law at Mount Sinai with thunder and lightning. He's on the throne, in control of the universe.

Notice the 24 thrones around the main one. There were 12 tribes of Israel and 12 disciples of Jesus: these 24 elders symbolise *all* God's people.

👁 **Read verses 6–11**

▶ *What were these weird creatures doing? (v8)*

▶ *And the elders? (v9)*

▶ *What are the reasons for bowing down to God? (v11)*

The four fantastic creatures symbolise the world that God has created. One day, the whole world — everything God has made — will worship Him.

THINK IT OVER

In this amazing vision, John is shown the world from the perspective of heaven: God's in complete control. Think how this would have encouraged Christians in the seven churches who were under attack for their beliefs.

▶ *How is it an encouragement to you too?*

THE BOTTOM LINE

God's on His throne. King forever.

➔ **TAKE IT FURTHER**

More explanation on page 113.

20 | Lion or lamb?

Ready for more of John's vision of the heavenly throne room? It involves a hard-to-open scroll, a lion, a lamb, and all those animals and elders again. Remember, Revelation is revealing the real Jesus to us.

👁 Read Revelation 5 v 1–5

ENGAGE YOUR BRAIN
▷ *Why is John blubbing? (v4)*

▷ *What stopped his tears? (v5)*

The scroll contains God's plan for world history. Until it's opened, God's plan to act in rescue and judgment remains unknown and uncompleted. But the Lion of Judah (Jesus) can open it. So get ready for this roaring lion...

👁 Read verses 6–10
▷ *What does John see instead of a lion? (v6)*

▷ *What happened when He took the scroll? (v8)*

▷ *How would you summarise their new song? (v9–10)*

Jesus is pictured as both the lion (to show His total authority) and the lamb (to show He laid down His life

for people in sacrificial service). Jesus' death is central to everything.

👁 Read verses 11–14
Thousands and thousands of angels giving Jesus the praise He deserves for dying in our place.

PRAY ABOUT IT
If you agree with the angels' words, make a point of honouring Jesus in your own words right now.

THE BOTTOM LINE
Jesus' death is central to the whole of history.

→ TAKE IT FURTHER
More stuff on page 113.

21 Dark riders

Now we get to the juicy stuff you've been waiting for: the four horsemen of the apocolypse, souls of the dead, earthquakes, the moon turning blood red, stars falling from the sky. Terrifying, but essential stuff.

Read Revelation 6 v 1–8

We've now reached the first series of events describing history between Christ's resurrection and return.

ENGAGE YOUR BRAIN

▶ *What picture do we get?*

The white horse = aggressive military regimes; red horse = war; black horse = famine that follows war; pale horse = death that follows famine and war.

▶ *What shows that these things are in Jesus' control? (v2, v4, v8)*

▶ *How is this truth supported by v1, 3, 5 and 7?*

Read verses 9–11

▶ *What extra suffering will some believers face? (v9)*

▶ *What will they ask? (v10)*

▶ *What will they be told? (v11)*

Read verses 12–17

▶ *How would you sum up the events described here?*

The first five seals are about human history before Jesus returns. The sixth seal brings God's judgment on the cruel, persecuting rulers we've been reading about in v1–11. The big question is in v17: *"The great day of their wrath has come, and who can stand?"* We'll discover the answer tomorrow.

PRAY ABOUT IT

Thank God that He's in control of our world, even when it doesn't seem like it. Thank Him that He looks after His people and their future with Him is totally secure.

→ TAKE IT FURTHER

Ride on to page 113.

22 | Making a stand

Yesterday we read about the terrifying things that would happen in the world before Jesus returns. It ended with the question: "The great day of their wrath has come, and who can stand?" Well, here's the answer...

👁 Read Revelation 7 v 1–10

▶ *Who will be safe? (v3)*

▶ *How are they described? (v9)*

▶ *And what did they recognise? (v10)*

Don't get hung up on the number 144,000. It's not to be taken literally — there are more Christians than that! From John's perspective, they're a huge crowd, too large to count (v9). From God's perspective, they total 144,000. That's best understood as representing the complete people of God (12 tribes of Israel x 12 apostles x 1000, the superlative number). The important fact is that God's people are all safe because Jesus has rescued them (v10).

👁 Read verses 11–17

▶ *How does John describe the huge crowd? (v14)*

▶ *What made their robes white?*

▶ *What's the great future for these people? (v15–16)*

▶ *Why and how? (v17)*

The "great tribulation" is a time of great suffering and persecution. These believers know from the pain of their sufferings that rescue is only found in God. They only have victory because of the blood of Jesus. Yes, Christians suffer in this life. But it's only for a very short time compared to an eternity living with God, under His protection. There will be no more hunger, thirst, tears or suffering.

THINK IT OVER

▶ *What encouragement is there for Christians when life gets hard?*
▶ *What future is there?*

PRAY ABOUT IT

What do you want to say to God today?

→ TAKE IT FURTHER

There's more on page 113.

23 | Incensed and fiery

More weird images and names now. But get the truths behind them. And remember that chapters 8–11 view the same period of history as chapters 6–7 (the time between Jesus' resurrection and His return), but from a new angle.

Read Revelation 8 v 1–6

ENGAGE YOUR BRAIN

▶ *What happened during the silence? (v3)*

A censer was filled with sweet-smelling incense, used during special ceremonies. But here it was filled with the prayers of Christians ("saints"). The angel was helping deliver these prayers. It's a great reminder that our prayers are never merely our own — the Holy Spirit helps us pray (Romans 8 v 16–17).

The prayers here were dramatically answered as the angel threw down fire on the earth: God is about to act in judgment...

Read verses 7–13

▶ *What effect do these judgments have on the world?*
v7:
v8–9:
v11:
v12:

▶ *And what was the warning? (v13)*

The first four trumpets bring disaster on the world. But this time it's nature that's affected — the earth, sea, rivers and skies. It seems as if human sin is the cause of this punishment, which is terrifying yet only partial — one third of the world affected. The worrying thing is that the next few trumpets will bring worse judgments (v13). But that comes tomorrow.

PRAY ABOUT IT

It's humans who have brought God's judgment on the world. What specific sins do you need to admit to God and repent of right now? Thank Him that He hasn't destroyed us and our world, even though we deserve it.

→ TAKE IT FURTHER

Eco warriors turn to page 114.

24 | Scorpion attack

So, four of the seven angels have blown trumpets and the world has been struck with natural disasters. Now for judgments five and six which affect humans more directly. Hope you're not scared of bugs.

👁 Read Revelation 9 v 1–12

ENGAGE YOUR BRAIN

▶ *Any ideas who the fallen star is? (v1, 11)*

▶ *Who was singled out for torture? (v4)*

▶ *How bad was it? (v5–6)*

The fallen star (also called Abaddon and Apollyon, which mean Destroyer) seems to be Satan. Yet any power he has is limited (v4–5) — God is the one in control. So the devil and evil forces will torment non-Christians for a while ("five months") but even that is limited.

👁 Read verses 13–21

▶ *What tragedy did the sixth trumpet announce? (v15)*

▶ *Yet what effect did it have on mankind? (v20–21)*

This time the evil armies *do* kill people — many people. Surely this would be recognised as punishment from God! But no, people continue to worship idols, steal, murder and sin sexually. People never seem to learn. The situation seems hopeless. But this isn't the end. We've had six of the seven angelic trumpets — so one remains. But you'll have to wait for that.

GET ON WITH IT

▶ *Who do you know who refuses to turn to God?*
▶ *How can you explain to them the seriousness of their decision?*
▶ *Which sins do you keep going back to despite what Jesus has done for you?*
▶ *How can you (with God's help) attack these sins in a new way?*

PRAY ABOUT IT

Whatever is on your heart and mind, take it to God right now.

→ TAKE IT FURTHER

For a sting in the tail, try page 114.

25 ¦ Sweet and sour

The first six trumpets brought God's judgment on the world, yet people ignored the warnings and carried on sinning. There's now a pause before the seventh and final trumpet is sounded.

👁 Read Revelation 10 v 1–4

ENGAGE YOUR BRAIN

▶ How is this new angel described? (v1, 3)
▶ What was he holding? (v2)
▶ What's the surprising instruction to John? (v4)

This angel's appearance and voice reminds us of God, so he seems to be speaking God's words, on His behalf. Yet John is told not to write them down. We'll never know what they were. If God has decided we shouldn't hear them, then it's best that we don't!

👁 Read verses 5–11

▶ What was John told to do next? (v8)
▶ In what contrasting ways is the scroll described? (v9)
▶ What else is John commanded to do? (v11)

The sixth trumpet has sounded, the end of the world and judgment are just around the corner, but before then there is a job to do. The giant angel has been carrying a little scroll, which John is told to eat. It tastes sweet in his mouth but disagrees with his stomach.

The word of God is sweet — great news to many. But it also has a bitter quality that many don't want to hear. The gospel includes the bitter truth of punishment for rejecting God as well as the sweet news of rescue for those who trust Jesus.

THINK IT OVER

▶ What experience have you had of the joy of the gospel?
▶ When has the gospel brought you rejection?
▶ How does chapter 10 encourage us to hang in there, in telling our friends about the gospel?

→ TAKE IT FURTHER
No *Take it further* today.

26 | Expert witness

Yesterday we read about the gospel message being both sweet and bitter. Well, today we'll discover just how hard to swallow some people find it. Get ready for more crazy imagery too.

👁 Read Revelation 11 v 1-6

ENGAGE YOUR BRAIN

▶ *What was John's task? (v1)*

▶ *What would happen to God's city? (v2)*

▶ *How will God make sure His message is heard? (v3, 5, 6)*

God's people would be trampled for a while (v2). The two witnesses stand for Christians who spread the message of Jesus. God will protect them and their message and it will have a powerful effect. Although this wouldn't last for ever.

👁 Read verses 7-14

▶ *What would happen to the witnesses? (v7)*

▶ *Whose side is the world on? (v8–10)*

▶ *But what would happen to them? (v13)*

▶ *What about the witnesses? (v11–12)*

This all seems to be pointing to a time

in history when the Christian message is ignored and appears to be defeated by Satan (v7). Many people see the message of Jesus as irritating and tormenting them and they'd love to see it defeated (v10). But when Jesus returns, His witnesses will be raised to live with Him and the gospel will be shown to be the truth. Christians can be killed but they can't be destroyed. They'll live for ever with Jesus.

👁 Read verses 15-19

▶ *What's the great news when Jesus returns? (v15)*

▶ *What will happen when He does? (v18)*

PRAY ABOUT IT

Pray for yourself, your church and other Christians, that you'll faithfully share the truth of the gospel despite opposition and rejection.

More from Revelation in a few weeks.

→ TAKE IT FURTHER

More on the weird stuff on page 114.

27 | City centre

Do you enjoy a good puzzle? Then try to work out what Psalm 87 is all about. It'll help to know that "Zion" was an Old Testament word for Jerusalem and that the names in v4 were all cities or countries.

👁 Read Psalm 87 v 1–3

ENGAGE YOUR BRAIN
▶ *What do we learn about God's city?*

God chose Jerusalem to be His special city during Old Testament times. It was called "holy" (v1) because God shared His presence with His people there. See what great things (v3) would be said about Jerusalem...

👁 Read verses 4–7

▶ *Who's doing the writing?*

▶ *What's being written down and where is it being written?*

▶ *What's incredible about all this?*

▶ *Who breaks into song and why? (v7)*

People from Rahab (Egypt), Babylon, Philistia, Tyre and Cush (Ethiopia) will all be recorded in God's book. That's incredible news — people from all nations (Jews *and* Gentiles) will enjoy the privilege of being God's people. And that includes you and me who trust Him too.

God's life ("fountain") flows within the city of His people. Revelation reminds us this is true not for earthly Jerusalem, but a heavenly one. The city of God in His new heavens and earth. It will be filled with His people — those who trust in His Son, Jesus.

THINK IT OVER
▶ *Do you look forward to living in this city?*
▶ *Why / why not?*

PRAY ABOUT IT
Talk to God about your feelings regarding the future with Him. Ask Him to get you excited about life in His perfect city.

→ TAKE IT FURTHER
Zechariah agrees on page 115.

The Bible's big story

THE BEGINNING

The Bible begins with God speaking the universe into existence (Genesis 1). Jesus was there right at the beginning: "All things were created by him and for him" (Colossians 1 v 16). Amazingly, the pinnacle of God's creation was human life. Men and women were designed in God's own image. They lived in the perfect place (Eden) in a perfect relationship with God.

But perfection didn't last long. Disguised as a snake, Satan persuaded Eve (and then Adam) to disobey God. They hoped eating the forbidden fruit would put them on God's level. So sin entered God's new world and messed it up. Humans wanted to rule their own lives and rejected God's rule. But they had to face the consequences — they were thrown out of God's presence and would now die. Sin polluted humanity. Every human is now born into a sinful world and will be guilty of his or her own sins. Our sins must be punished by eternal spiritual death. As the human race grew, sin spread.

GOD'S PEOPLE

It was always God's plan to provide a permanent sacrifice for the penalty of sin. As part of that plan, God selected a group of people to be His chosen nation. The Lord promised Abraham his descendants would become a great nation; they'd have their own land; and all mankind would be blessed by one of Abraham's descendants (Genesis 12 v 1–3). Despite Abaham's wife, Sarah, being 90 and infertile, God gave them a son, Isaac. God's promises were already being fulfilled.

Fast forward 500 years and the nation of Israel was now huge but they were slaves in Egypt. In an amazing picture of how God would rescue believers from sin, the Lord rescued His people from Egypt. At Mount Sinai, God gave Moses the 10 Commandments. The Lord promised to be with His people, protecting them and leading them to the promised land. In return, the Israelites must keep God's laws. But it became obvious the people couldn't do this as they repeatedly rebelled against God. They wanted to be bosses of their own lives.

GOD'S KINGDOM

As evidence of this self-reliance, God's people asked for a king to lead them instead of God. Later King David ruled Israel and served God. Israel became a great nation. But David wasn't perfect and God's people continued to disobey Him. Yet God promised a perfect King, who one day would lead God's people to an eternal promised land. The Lord sent messengers (prophets) to instruct His people to turn back to Him, but they continued to reject God and they were punished — their enemies dividing and scattering them. By the time Jesus was born, there was only a smallish community of Jews living in Judah. Things were not looking good for God's people.

GOD'S KING

But God never forgot His promises to Abraham. Jesus, the promised King, was born in the small town of Bethlehem. At the age of 30, Jesus began His public ministry, and His words had a huge impact. Stuff like "I am the way and the truth and the life. No one comes to the Father except through me" (John 14 v 6). His claims were unique. Many people believed Jesus but many rejected Him and some even plotted to kill Him. The way Jesus lived and the amazing miracles He did backed up His claims to be God's Son and the only way to get right with God. But the plot to murder Jesus succeeded (yet it was all in God's plan). This was

the big moment the whole Bible had been building up to. Jesus willingly accepted His fate. Jesus was the ultimate sacrifice. He died to take the punishment for our sin. And He didn't stay dead — He was raised back to life to beat sin and death for ever. All who trust in Jesus' awesome sacrifice can have eternal life with Him.

GOD'S MESSAGE SPREADS

Jesus appeared to many people after His resurrection. He told His disciples to spread the message of His salvation to the whole world. And He said one day He would return as Judge — to punish those who reject Him and gather believers to live with Him in His new kingdom. After the Gospels, the rest of the New Testament describes Jesus' followers spreading the message and many lives being changed. Jesus gave His Spirit to help all believers serve Him and spread the gospel. The New T also has loads of letters packed with vital truths about Jesus and living for Him. Together, they're like a manual for how to live as a Christian.

The final book of the Bible, Revelation, tells us (in futuristic picture language) the whole story of God's plan. It also talks about God's plan for Jesus to return as Judge and about the new heavens and earth, where all believers will live with God in perfection: the new Eden. And that's the story of the Bible. It's all about Jesus.

2 Samuel

Kingdom come

The story so far: God's people were in the land, Canaan, that God had promised them. But things weren't rosy: His people seemed stubbornly intent on living without Him. Yet God answered their insulting request for a king.

The first king, Saul, didn't live God's way. So God chose David to replace him. But the handover wasn't immediate and it was very messy. At the end of 1 Samuel, Saul finally died. Asking *"What happened next?"* will reveal some surpising twists and turns. We'll warn you now that the 2 Samuel story gets pretty grubby: human pride and arrogance lead to some sordid events.

In 2 Samuel we'll learn a lot about God and His people and how badly we humans treat Him. We'll also look at what this bloodthirsty soap opera of a story teaches about God. Look for signs and clues along the way.

Asking *"What does the story show God is like?"* will whack home to us how great the Lord is.

We'll also see what 2 Samuel shows us about God's great plan. Asking *"So what does the story teach about God's purposes?"* will point us forward to Jesus. Come and make the link between the kingdom of David and a far greater kingdom to come.

Get ready for civil war, double-crossing, murder (lots of it), battles, big promises, lust, adultery, more wars, rape, conspiracy, rebellion, revenge, mighty warriors and some huge life lessons.

28 ┆ A sad start ┆

God had chosen David to replace Saul as king over His people, Israel. And, at last, Saul was now dead. But how would David take the news?

👁 **Read 2 Samuel 1 v 1–16**

ENGAGE YOUR BRAIN

▷ *What was the terrible news? (v4)*
▷ *Who brought the news? (v2, 13)*
▷ *What did he claim to have done? (v10)*
▷ *How did David and his men react to the news? (v12)*
▷ *What happened to the Amalekite? (v15)*
▷ *Why? (v14, 16)*

This bad news boy was lying. Saul fell on his own sword (1 Samuel 31 v 4). This Amalekite travelled for days to bring this news and claim to have killed Saul, probably hoping for a top job with the new king, David. King Saul had hunted David for years and tried to kill him, but Saul was God's anointed king so David and his men mourned Saul's death.

👁 **Read verses 17–27**

▷ *What gets repeated throughout this sad song?*

▷ *Which verses show David's... big heartedness towards Saul?*

friendship with Jonathan?

desire for God's honour?

concern for His people?

David didn't gloat over his rival's death. He mourned that God's chosen king was dead and that Israel's (and therefore God's) glory was in tatters (v19). Their enemies seemed to be winning and his best friend Jonathan was dead. No wonder David was in floods of tears.

PRAY ABOUT IT

Do you care more for your own success or wellbeing or for God's glory and His people? Ask God to help you sort your priorities out as you read 2 Samuel.

→ **TAKE IT FURTHER**

An overview of 2 Sam is on page 115.

29 | Tribal trouble

King Saul's dead. So, time for David to take the throne, right? Er well, not quite yet. Things are never that simple. Step forward Abner and Ish-Bosheth to get in David's way.

👁 Read 2 Samuel 2 v 1–7

ENGAGE YOUR BRAIN

▶ What did God tell David to do? (v1)

▶ What great thing happened in Hebron? (v4)

▶ What had the men of Jabesh Gilead done?

▶ What was the great result for them? (v5–6)

So David was officially king at last! But only of Judah, just one of the twelve tribes of Israel.

👁 Read verses 8–23

▶ Who was king of Israel? (v10)

▶ What army commander Abner's role in this? (v8–9)

After Ish-Bosheth was made king, civil war broke out. Abner led his army into David's territory for a fight. Joab headed up David's army and was pretty good at it.

👁 Read 2 v 24 – 3 v 5

▶ How did the battle come to a head? (v24–25)

▶ How did Abner persuade Joab to call off the chase? (v26–28)

▶ Who came out on top in the battle? (v30–31)

▶ And what continued to happen? (3 v 1)

Abner knew that God had chosen David as king, so he was openly going against God's rule and wanting to impose his own authority. And when we refuse to obey God as the ruler of our lives, we're doing the same thing.

PRAY ABOUT IT

Pray for people you know (maybe yourself) who refuse to accept God as king of their lives.

→ TAKE IT FURTHER

A glimpse into the future on p115.

30 ¦ Switching sides

Abner had been commander of King Saul's army. Despite knowing David was God's choice for king, he backed Saul's son Ish-Bosheth and fought against David's army, which was led by Joab. But get ready for a suprise or two.

👁 Read 2 Samuel 3 v 6–11

ENGAGE YOUR BRAIN

- ▶ *What had Abner been doing? (v6)*
- ▶ *What did the king accuse him of? (v7)*
- ▶ *What was Abner's shock response? (v8–10)*

Ish-Bosheth was getting paranoid and accused Abner of sleeping with one of his father's women. Such an act was equivalent to claiming the throne. Abner knew that I-B was calling him a "dog's head" — a traitor. So Abner switched sides to join his former enemies.

👁 Read verses 12–21

- ▶ *What deal did Abner strike with David? (v12–13)*
- ▶ *What did Abner do on David's behalf? (v17, 19)*
- ▶ *What did he remind the elders? (v18)*

👁 Read verse 22–39

- ▶ *What was Joab's response to Abner moving in on his territory? (v24–27)*
- ▶ *What was his reason? (v30)*
- ▶ *But how did David react to Abner's death? (v31–36)*
- ▶ *What did he want everyone to know? (v37)*

Abner wanted power and respect. Joab wanted authority and revenge. David wanted all of Israel to accept him as king. There's hardly any mention of God in this story.

THINK IT OVER

- ▶ *Do you make decisions based on what you'll get out of it or what God wants with your life?*

PRAY ABOUT IT

Ask God to remind you of your need to put Him first and not your own selfish ambition.

→ TAKE IT FURTHER

No *Take it further* today.

31 ┆ King at last

David refused to murder his way to the top. After all, God had promised he would be king, so there was no need to hurry God's timing. Not everyone took that view though.

👁 Read 2 Samuel 4 v 1–12

ENGAGE YOUR BRAIN

▸ *What happened in Israel after Abner's murder? (v1)*

▸ *What did Recab and Baanah claim was the reason for the murdering the king? (v8)*

▸ *How did David see it? (v11–12)*

These two violent bandits horribly murdered Israel's king and then claimed it was God getting revenge on David's behalf! But David knew what was going on and rightly punished Recab and Baanah for killing Ish-Bosheth. God would keep him safe without using murderous criminals (v9).

THINK IT OVER

▸ *Do you ever claim to be serving God when you're only serving yourself?*

👁 Read 2 Samuel 5 v 1–5

▸ *Why were the people happy to have David as their king? (v1–2)*

At last, David was king over all Israel — all of God's people. They remembered how he'd successfully led them in battle many times and that God had chosen him to be king. Many years earlier, the Lord had promised this to David. Many times it had seemed impossible, but God always keeps His promises.

PRAY ABOUT IT

Thank the Lord that He is completely trustworthy. Now think of specific times you've seen His promises to be true and thank Him. Pray that you will serve God wholeheartedly for all the right reasons.

TAKE IT FURTHER

Feeling sheepish? Turn to page 115.

32 Conquering king

David is finally king of all Israel. So life will be much more peaceful now, right? Er, no. He's still got to capture Jerusalem and an enemy army is getting ready for a fight.

Read 2 Samuel 5 v 6–16

ENGAGE YOUR BRAIN

- *What did the people in Jerusalem claim? (v6)*
- *What happened? (v7)*
- *What was Jerusalem's new name? (v9)*
- *Why was David successful? (v10)*
- *Why was David confident about? (v12)*
- *Yet what did he do? (v13)*

All of this tells us a lot about David's reign as king. He was God's chosen king who lived God's way. All his success and power was down to the Lord. And yet we get a glimpse of David's weakness. He was still a sinful human and his soft spot for women (v13) would bring trouble later on.

Read verses 17–25

- *How did the Philistines react to David becoming king? (v17)*
- *What did David do first? (v19, 23)*
- *What happened both times? (v20, 25)*

The last thing the Philistines wanted was Israel united under one king, so they attacked. But David's army, following God's battle plans, defeated them twice. God's promise to protect David and His people was already being kept.

God protects His people! He does this by guiding them, so we should ask Him to lead us in life. He also does it by His great power. Whatever we face in life, Christians must never forget that God is with them, His plans never fail and He's stronger than any opposition.

PRAY ABOUT IT

Thank God that He guides and protects His people. Now tell Him about any worries or opposition you face currently, and ask for His help.

THE BOTTOM LINE

God saves and protects His people.

→ TAKE IT FURTHER

More stuff on page 115.

33 ┊ Fear and loathing in Jerusalem

Remember the ark of God, ark of the covenant? It was a box containing the 10 Commandments. It represented God's actual presence among His people. They were God's people and He lived among them. Special stuff.

👁 Read 2 Samuel 6 v 1–11

ENGAGE YOUR BRAIN
▶ *Why do you think David wanted the ark back?*
▶ *But what went wrong? (v6)*
▶ *How serious was this? (v7)*
▶ *What were David's two reactions? v8:*
v9–10:

It's hard to imagine how important the ark was — this box represented the very presence of mighty God among His people. That's why David wanted it with him. But it's also why Uzzah was killed for showing God no respect. God is holy and perfect; we can't take Him lightly.

👁 Read verses 12–23
▶ *Why did David change his mind? (v12)*
▶ *What did David do to celebrate the ark's return? (v13–19)*
▶ *What upset Michal? (v16, 20)*
▶ *What did David say? (v21)*

God's presence was something to be celebrated. It brought Obed-Edom great blessing and (most of) the people of Jerusalem were excited to have God's ark back with them. Michal, however, was more bothered about the king being so unkingly and dancing around. But David had the right perspective — it didn't matter what other people thought; he was dancing for *God*.

GET ON WITH IT
▶ *How do you fail to show God the fear and respect He deserves?*
▶ *When do you care more about what other people think than what God thinks?*
▶ *What can you do about these things?*

PRAY ABOUT IT
Talk to God about anything He's challenged you about today.

TAKE IT FURTHER
More ark antics on page 115.

34 Home sweet home

David was worried: he had a lovely huge new palace but God only had a tent (well, that's what the ark was kept in). It just didn't seem right.

👁 Read 2 Samuel 7 v 1–11

ENGAGE YOUR BRAIN

▷ What does v2 tell us about David's attitude to God?
▷ What did God say about the idea? (v5–7)
▷ What had God done for David in the past? (v8–9)
▷ What would He do for David in the future?
  v9:
  v10:
  v11:

It was right that David wanted the best for God, but it would be David's son Solomon who built a temple for God. For now, David could enjoy reflecting on all the amazing stuff God had done for him, and look forward to God's promises for the future — David would be known as a great man, and the Israelites would finally have a secure home, with rest from their enemies.

👁 Read verses 12–17

▷ What would happen after David's death? (v12)
▷ Who does v13–15 remind you of?

Promises beyond David's wildest imagination: he wasn't to build a house for God, but God told David his "house" (kingdom) would last for ever. God would treat the king on David's throne like a father treats a son, with discipline, in love (v14–15). The New Testament tells us Jesus was born into David's family. He's the King who'll rule for ever.

THINK IT OVER

▷ What's brilliant about God and His promises?
▷ Why can we trust Him?

PRAY ABOUT IT

Tell God your response. And we'll catch David's tomorrow.

→ TAKE IT FURTHER

Move house to page 116.

35 | Prayers and promises

David offered to build God a house but he could never have expected what came next. God chose to tell David about His plan for eternity, saying that David's "house" would last and last. And that blew David apart...

👁 Read 2 Samuel 7 v 18–24

ENGAGE YOUR BRAIN

▶ *What does David repeatedly call God?*

▶ *What does that mean?*

▶ *And what does he call himself? (v19, 20, 21)*

▶ *What had God done for His people? (v23–24)*

God is sovereign — He's in control of everything. David is shocked and amazed that God has shared His future plans with David and promised him so much. This great eternal future is promised to God's people. No wonder David wants to sing God's praise and is happy to be His servant.

👁 Read verses 25–29

▶ *What did David want most of all? (v26)*

▶ *Why did David believe God's promise? (v22–24)*

THINK IT OVER

Think how these reminders about God's character and purposes might affect your outlook today.

▶ *Why should we, like David, be impressed by God?*

▶ *Why should we trust Him?*

PRAY ABOUT IT

Now praise God, thank Him and renew your trust in Him and His Son Jesus, the great son of David.

THE BOTTOM LINE

God keeps His promises and that gives us confidence to pray.

TAKE IT FURTHER

More prayer pointers on page 116.

36 | Winning ways

God promised David rest from his enemies. But that wouldn't happen suddenly: it would come from vicious battles, with God leading His people to victory.

👁 Read 2 Samuel 8 v 1–6

ENGAGE YOUR BRAIN

- 🔽 *Who did David defeat first? (v1)*
- 🔽 *What did he do to the Moabites?*
- 🔽 *And what about Hadadezer's chariots and horses?*
- 🔽 *What happened to the Arameans? (v6)*
- 🔽 *Why do you think David was so ruthless?*

God had made David king of all Israel, so all around his kingdom David established control. All of these enemy armies refused to let God's king be in charge, so rightly David defeated them. God was in charge of Israel, with David as His king.

👁 Read verses 7–14

- 🔽 *What did David grab from the defeated enemies? (v7–8)*
- 🔽 *And what did they give him as gifts? (v10)*
- 🔽 *What did David do with all this stuff? (v11)*

David was king, but God was in charge, so David handed over all the best stuff to God.

GET ON WITH IT

- 🔽 *Do you give God what rightly belongs to Him?*
- 🔽 *How can you devote more of your money to God?*
- 🔽 *How could you use possessions to serve God?*
- 🔽 *What about your talents and abilities?*

PRAY ABOUT IT

Thank God that He's in complete control. Thank Him that even though life can be tough, Jesus has already won the ultimate victory for His people and they will celebrate with Him in the new Jerusalem.

TAKE IT FURTHER

The lowdown on v15–18 is on p116.

37 | Last man standing

Kings often wiped out any living relatives of the monarch they'd taken over from. They were worried that such relatives might claim the throne or have them assassinated. Saul's grandson was still alive...

👁 Read 2 Samuel 9 v 1–7

ENGAGE YOUR BRAIN

▶ *What do we learn about Saul's grandson? (v4)*

▶ *What was surprising about the way David treated him? (v7)*

▶ *What was David's reason? (v7)*

Saul's son Jonathan had been David's best friend. David promised always to show kindness to Jonathan's family (1 Samuel 20). Many years later, David kept his word. David took his covenant with Jonathan very seriously. Not only did he spare Mephibosheth's life, he promised him great things. And that's the way God treats His people — He keeps His promises and lavishes great things on them.

👁 Read verses 8–13

▶ *What did Mephibosheth call himself? (v8)*

▶ *Why might he feel like that? (v13)*

▶ *Yet what did David do for him? (v9–11)*

Mephibosheth had a major disability *and* was Saul's grandson, so should have been an enemy of David. But because of David's promise to Jonathan, Meph received far more than he ever could have hoped for. This is all a great picture of God's love for undeserving rebels like us. Romans 5 v 8 puts it perfectly: *"But God demonstrates his own love for us in this: While we were still sinners, Christ died for us."*

GET ON WITH IT

▶ *If God shows you such undeserved love, who do you need to show similar love to?*

▶ *How will you do this?*

PRAY ABOUT IT

Loads to thank God for today.

→ TAKE IT FURTHER

No *Take it further* today.

38 The cheek of it!

Have you ever had your good intentions thrown back in your face? Maybe you tried to be nice to someone but they misunderstood your motives and assumed you were out to get them.

👁 **Read 2 Samuel 10 v 1–5**

ENGAGE YOUR BRAIN
▶ *What did David do and why?*
▶ *What did the Ammonites think was really going on? (v3)*
▶ *What was their reaction? (v4)*

It was pretty classy of David to send his condolences when the king of a rival tribe died. But the Ammonites panicked and humiliated David's men. Imagine having half your beard shaved off and your clothes ripped so your buttocks were showing! What an insult! And a very bad move...

👁 **Read verses 6–12**

▶ *What did the Ammonites do next? (v6)*
▶ *And David's response? (v7)*
▶ *What was Joab's response to being surrrounded? (v12)*

What a brilliant attitude! Fighting bravely for God and His people; knowing that whatever happens, God is in charge; doing the right thing.

GET ON WITH IT
▶ *How can you make more of a stand for God and His people?*
▶ *What worries do you need to hand over to Him, trusting His perfect plans?*

Talk to God about these things.

👁 **Read verses 13–19**

▶ *What happened? (v14)*
▶ *And then what? (v17–18)*
▶ *What was the great result for David and Israel? (v19)*

Yet again, God led His people to a spectacular victory. At last, Israel was united and at peace, under God's chosen king, David. But tomorow we'll see that it was not the end of David's problems.

PRAY ABOUT IT
"The Lord will do what is good in his sight."

→ **TAKE IT FURTHER**
Close-up on Joab on page 116.

39 | Home alone

Adultery. Attempted cover-up. Murder. Lies.
All in chapter 11. Who is it who's sunk to this
degrading behaviour? Er, King David. Here's
the whole sordid story.

👁 Read 2 Samuel 11 v 1–13

ENGAGE YOUR BRAIN

- ▶ *Where was David and where should he have been? (v1)*
- ▶ *What was his big mistake? (v4)*
- ▶ *What was the result?*
- ▶ *How did David try to cover it up? (v8–13)*

Notice how David fell into his sin:
v1: he wasn't doing what he should have been doing;
v2: he let his eyes wander and linger;
v3: he let his desire grow stronger until he couldn't control it.

THINK IT OVER

- ▶ *How will you stop a glance becoming a gaze?*
- ▶ *Are you at risk when you're just killing time?*

👁 Read verses 14–27

- ▶ *How did David and Joab plot Uriah's death? (v14–17)*
- ▶ *How did Bathsheba react? (v26)*
- ▶ *What did David do? (v27)*

▶ *How did God feel about it? (v27)*

David lusted after another man's wife and slept with her. She fell pregnant so David had the unfortunate husband killed and then took Bathsheba and her son into his palace. Nasty stuff. But the bottom line is this: *"David had ... displeased the Lord"* (v27). David told Joab to get over Uriah's death (v25), but God wouldn't just let it go. The story continues tomorrow.

PRAY ABOUT IT

Sin can take hold of us bit by bit without us realising. Talk to God about specific temptations you struggle with. Ask Him to help you fight sin off at its earliest stages.

→ TAKE IT FURTHER

The different sides of David can be seen on page 116.

40 Twist in the tale

Tick tick tick... time passed. Bathsheba became David's wife. Their son was born. Surely life could now just carry on. But God's clock was ticking too and it was time for the alarm to go off. David would get a rude awakening.

Read 2 Samuel 12 v 1–9

ENGAGE YOUR BRAIN

- How did David react to Nathan's little lamb story? (v5–6)
- What was the twist in the tale? (v7)
- What had God done for David? (v7–8)
- Yet what had David done in return? (v9)

Read verses 10–14

- How would God punish David? (v10)
- How else? (v11–12)
- How else and why? (v14)
- How did God show David great kindness? (v13)

David admitted his sin and God granted him immediate forgiveness — he was spared the death penalty he deserved. David was forgiven but he would still have to face the consequences of his sin.

Read verses 15–25

- What tragedy did David suffer because of his sin? (v15, 18)
- What shocked David's servants? (v21)
- How did David explain his actions? (v22–23)
- How did God show more amazing kindness to David? (v24–25)

Despite God's punishment, David still knew how gracious God could be. That's why he kept praying for his sick son. On this occasion, God said no to David's prayers. But God then gave David another son, who the Lord loved. Even David's sin was used by God as part of His plans — Solomon would inherit David's throne and build God's temple.

THE BOTTOM LINE

David experienced a shattering truth: that God forgives those who admit their wrong against Him.

→ TAKE IT FURTHER

Missing verses found on page 117.

Why do I keep sinning?

That familiar sensation of shame, anger at yourself and frustration comes over you. Why did I say that? Why couldn't I keep my mouth shut? How did I let myself end up on that website AGAIN? Why can't I have more self-control? It's just too hard to stop... Lord, why do I keep sinning???

THE POWER OF SIN

Surely once you've become a Christian, you've been rescued from sin, haven't you? Romans 4 v 16 says: *"Sin shall not be your master"*. But hang on — 1 John 1 v 8 tells us: *"If we claim to be without sin, we deceive ourselves and the truth is not in us"*. It's confusing. But let's try to get our heads around what the Bible teaches on sin and our battle with it.

When Jesus died on the cross, He took the punishment we all deserve for our sin. When we trust in His death in our place, we are freed from the power of sin. It might not feel like it as we struggle against swearing, lustful thoughts or the self-centred tendency to leave God out of our lives — but we are no longer slaves to sin. Go and read the whole of Romans chapter 6... go on!

A NEW MASTER

You might not think of yourself as a slave (v16) but the Bible is very clear — you are either a slave to sin or a slave to righteousness, to God. Imagine you grew up supporting Manchester United soccer team and even ended up being signed by them and playing for them. But then a huge transfer fee is paid and you are bought by their rivals Chelsea. Your old loyalties have to end — you are part of a new club now; you have a new master.

Christians have a new master — Jesus Christ. We might fall back into our old patterns of behaviour sometimes, but we no longer blindly go with the flow. We don't want to sin. The tricky thing about becoming a Christian is learning to live as followers of Christ. As Ephesians 4 v 1 puts it: *"Live a*

life worthy of the calling you have received".

A LIFETIME'S BATTLE

The minute we trust in Jesus for forgiveness, we are forgiven. Spotless. Perfect. As Jesus takes our sin on Himself, we receive His righteousness (2 Corinthians 5 v 21). But in terms of our behaviour, it will take a lifetime before we reach perfection and live with God in His new creation. Before then, we must work hard at becoming more and more like Jesus.

It's not easy; in fact, it's painful. The Bible calls it "putting to death" our old self. But we're not alone in this struggle: God gives us His Holy Spirit. Romans 8 v 5–17 spells out the big difference this makes. The fact that you struggle against sin is a sign of the new life and hope you now have!

FREEDOM FROM SIN

We may be free from the punishment and power of sin, but we're not yet free from its presence. That should come as no shock. The news on TV, our neighbourhoods, even our homes are full of sin. It's hardly surprising that when we're surrounded by sin we sometimes get swept along with it. But there will come a day when the presence of sin is removed forever. Take a look at Revelation 21 v 22–27: nothing impure will ever enter God's wonderful new creation.

So be realistic. Look again at 1 John 1 v 8–9: *"If we claim to be without sin, we deceive ourselves and the truth is not in us. If we confess our sins, he is faithful and just and will forgive us our sins and purify us from all unrighteousness"*. Thank the Lord for freeing you from sin's penalty, ask for His help in purifying you day by day, and thank Him that the future will be free from sin for ever.

Some helpful books to read: Battles Christians Face – Vaughan Roberts; The Enemy Within – Kris Lundgaard. Both are available from www.thegoodbook.co.uk

41 | Matthew: The big picture

Back to Jesus teaching on the hillside. A bit of a mind-bender today; Jesus tells us He didn't come to abolish the Law but to fulfil it. What's that mean? Surely Christians today don't have to keep the Old Testament Law?

👁 Read Matthew 5 v 17–18

The Law and the Prophets means the Old Testament. One of the best ways to understand "fulfil" is that Jesus "filled it full" — He made it 3D. All the pictures and prophecies were pointing to Him. He completed the Old Testament; He gave it its full meaning.

👁 Read verses 19–20

ENGAGE YOUR BRAIN

▷ What's your first reaction to these verses?

▷ How can we meet the standards Jesus sets in v20?

Verse 20 would have sounded impossible — the Pharisees and teachers of the law were seen as super-holy — so how can anyone be more righteous than that? But the Pharisees actually reduced the law to a set of rules to keep. Over the next few days, Jesus will show us that true righteousness goes much deeper than that. And no one can keep the law perfectly... except Jesus. The only way we can be "righteous" is to be "in Christ" — to be saved by Him so that God treats us like His Son.

Jesus is the answer to the Old Testament, the final piece in the jigsaw. It points to Him. It's completed in Him. He's the one with ultimate, universal authority. And He says entering God's kingdom isn't about keeping laws, but looking to Jesus.

PRAY ABOUT IT

Thank God that if you are a Christian you are "in Christ" and His righteousness is your own.

THE BOTTOM LINE

Jesus came to fulfil the Law.

→ TAKE IT FURTHER

The bigger picture is on page 117.

42 Killer instinct

Jesus starts to explain what He means by fulfilling the Law now as He shows us the principles that the Law was designed to reflect. The first one is a real killer.

👁 Read Matthew 5 v 21–22

ENGAGE YOUR BRAIN

▶ *What rule did the Pharisees and teachers of the law teach? (v21)*

▶ *How is Jesus' command more demanding? (v22)*

▶ *Have you ever been guilty of breaking the Pharisees' rule?*

▶ *What about Jesus' command?*

Murdered anyone recently? No? How about being really angry with someone? Ah... Jesus isn't interested in merely keeping the rules; He wants our hearts to be right. His kingdom is about far more than looking OK and being religious.

PRAY ABOUT IT

Say sorry to God now for the times when you have murdered someone in your heart.

👁 Read verses 23–26

▶ *Offering a gift to God at the altar was serious stuff. What does Jesus say is more important?*

So, when you remember (maybe when you're in a Christian meeting) that a friend is upset with you, what's the only appropriate action? OK, it might interrupt the meeting, but get the point? It's got to be immediate.

GET ON WITH IT

Anyone you need to make peace with? Do it. RIGHT NOW!!!

THE BOTTOM LINE

God's as serious about anger in His disciples as He is about murder. So mend broken friendships. Now.

→ TAKE IT FURTHER

Kill some bad habits on page 117.

43 Serious sex stuff

Adultery sounds old-fashioned these days, unless we call it an affair. And divorce is just part of life now, isn't it? What have such topics got to do with you? A lot more than you think, says Jesus.

👁 **Read Matthew 5 v 27–32**

ENGAGE YOUR BRAIN

▶ *What rule did the Pharisees and teachers of the law teach? (v27)*

▶ *How is Jesus' command more demanding? (v28)*

▶ *Have you ever been guilty of breaking the Pharisees' rule?*

▶ *What about Jesus' command?*

When God gave the Ten Commandments to Moses, He wasn't just saying: "Don't commit adultery". He was reminding His people that marriage is special, that He is a loving, promise-keeping, faithful God and His people should be like Him. The Pharisees are reducing this heart attitude to a series of rules they can claim to keep or bend (v31). Jesus is having none of it.

▶ *How seriously does Jesus take our sin? (v29–30)*

▶ *Where is our sin really located? Hand? Eye? (Hint: v28)*

PRAY ABOUT IT

- Pray for the married couples you know, that God would bless them and help the husbands and wives to keep their marriage promises.
- Pray for people you know who have gone through the pain of divorce that they would know the comfort of God, who always keeps His promises.
- Pray for yourself that God would enable you to be pure in heart in your relationships with the opposite sex.

THE BOTTOM LINE

Take your sin seriously.

→ TAKE IT FURTHER

Dig deeper on page 117.

Yes = yes? Eye = eye?

Some slightly more unusual rules now — we don't spend much time swearing oaths these days unless we're in court. Although we all make promises. And what about grudges and taking vengeance?

👁 Read Matthew 5 v 33–37

ENGAGE YOUR BRAIN

▶ What rule did the Pharisees and teachers of the law teach? (v33)

▶ How is Jesus' command more demanding? (v37)

▶ Have you ever been guilty of breaking the Pharisees' rule?

▶ What about Jesus' command?

Are you a man/woman of your word? Do you keep your promises? Can people trust you when you say you'll do something?

👁 Read verses 38–42

▶ What's the Old Testament rule in v38?

▶ How is Jesus' command even harder? (v39–42)

▶ How did Jesus live out the principles of v39?

It's one thing to react proportionally to someone who wrongs you — she broke my pen so I'll take hers. That seems fair. But Jesus takes things to a whole different level. Christians will be wronged and persecuted and we must take it (v39). We should share our stuff generously (v42) and go out of our way for others (v41). After all, Jesus gave His life for us, so we should show His attitude to people around us.

TALK IT OVER

Get hold of another Christian and talk about whether v39 applies when we see people doing evil to others. Why? Why not? How would you back up your argument from the Bible?

THE BOTTOM LINE

Let your yes be yes and your no be no.

→ TAKE IT FURTHER

Eye up what's on page 117.

45 Love your enemies

By now the message is sinking in. God doesn't want us to be good, He wants us to be perfect! And we're not. Problem?

👁 Read Matthew 5 v 43–48

ENGAGE YOUR BRAIN

▶ *What rule did the Pharisees and teachers of the law teach? (v43)*

▶ *Is that easy to do?*

▶ *How is Jesus' command more demanding? (v44)*

▶ *Is that easy?*

One of the distinctive things about Christians is their ability to love their enemies. Just as Jesus prayed on the cross for those crucifying Him: "Father forgive them", Christians who were in concentration camps or who have had their families murdered have been able to forgive, pray for and love their enemies.

▶ *What is your reaction to Jesus' command in v48?*

▶ *How can we meet the standards which Jesus sets in v20 and v48?*

We can't. That's the simple answer. We're not perfect. But that's the whole point! Remember Matthew 5 v 3: *"Blessed are the poor in spirit for theirs is the kingdom of heaven!"* We have nothing to offer God; we can only accept what His Son has done. Jesus is perfect; He fulfils the Law and His heart is pure. Everything we have been reading about in chapter 5 that we can't do, He can!

PRAY ABOUT IT

Thank Jesus for all He's done on your behalf. Pray for specific people you find hard to love. Thank God that He loves them and ask for His help to be truly loving towards them.

THE BOTTOM LINE

Be perfect as your heavenly Father is perfect. In Christ, you are!

→ TAKE IT FURTHER

More top tips on page 118.

46 Godly giving

Being part of God's kingdom is about being pure in heart and not merely obeying rules. Jesus now tackles our sinful human desire to look as if we're holy on the outside when our motives are all wrong on the inside.

👁 Read Matthew 6 v 1–4

ENGAGE YOUR BRAIN

▶ *What is the headline warning for this next section, according to Jesus? (v1)*

▶ *What is the first example He gives of how we might do this? (v2)*

▶ *What is the danger we might fall into when giving money away?*

Jesus is warning us of the dangers of hypocrisy. A hypocrite is someone who says one thing and does another, or whose life doesn't match up with what they claim about it. The word originally meant "actor", and it's very easy to play the part of a Christian without being different on the inside.

GET ON WITH IT

▶ *Do you give to charities/people in need?*

▶ *What will you start doing?*

▶ *How might you be tempted to be hypocritical when giving money or time to good works?*

▶ *Where do we look for approval?*

▶ *Where should we want our reward to come from? (v4)*

PRAY ABOUT IT

Ask for God's help to have pure motives when giving money or time to help others. Use Psalm 139 v 23–24 and 2 Corinthians 8 v 7–9 to help you pray.

THE BOTTOM LINE

Beware of publicising your good deeds in front of others.

→ TAKE IT FURTHER

More warnings on page 118.

47 | How to pray

Jesus is warning us not to be hypocrites or boast about good stuff we do. What other "religious" activities might we be tempted to show off about? How about prayer?

👁 Read Mattthew 6 v 5-15

ENGAGE YOUR BRAIN

▷ What marked out a hypocrite's prayer in Jesus' day? (v5)
▷ How might a hypocrite pray today?
▷ How should our praying be different, according to Jesus?
▷ Look at v5–6. How are these two rewards different?
▷ Why don't we need to repeat certain "magic" words, phrases or mantras when we pray? (v7–8)

It's hard for us today to understand just how revolutionary it was for Jesus to say that God is our Father, who hears us and cares about our needs. The example of how to pray that He gives us in verses 9–13 is so familiar but is a brilliant way to help us pray.

PRAY ABOUT IT

Use the Lord's Prayer now to help you pray. After each line add in your own prayers on that topic:

Our Father in heaven, hallowed be your name,

Your kingdom come,

Your will be done, on earth as it is in heaven.

Give us today our daily bread.

And forgive us our debts, as we also have forgiven our debtors.

And lead us not into temptation, but deliver us from the evil one.

→ TAKE IT FURTHER
More prayer pointers on page 118.

48 | Banking on God

We've seen how easily we can be tempted to do things for the approval of others, rather than God. And now we see a fresh temptation — to put our trust and energies into something other than God.

👁 **Read Matthew 6 v 16–18**

ENGAGE YOUR BRAIN

▶ Although not many of us do it, fasting is something Jesus assumes Christians will do. What should fasting be about?

When you miss a meal to spend extra time with God or to help others, don't let anyone know. Just do life as normal (v17) and God will reward you with a closer relationship with Him.

GET ON WITH IT

Is fasting something you've ever thought about doing? It might not just be food. Maybe you could fast from social networking, or the internet or TV or gaming for a while so you can focus on prayer instead?

👁 **Read Matthew 6 v 19–24**

▶ List some of the ways we might "store up treasures on earth":

·

·

·

·

·

·

▶ What is the heart attitude behind storing up earthly treasures?

▶ How can we store up treasure in heaven?

▶ What is the problem Jesus highlights in v24?

We can't put all our trust in money and God at the same time — it's like having one foot in a boat and the other on the shore: sooner or later you'll end up doing the splits or falling into the water!

THE BOTTOM LINE

You can't serve both God and money.

→ **TAKE IT FURTHER**

Heart to heart — page 118.

49 | Why worry?

Trusting God is the foundation of our faith. We've seen how money and possessions can erode our trust in God, and now Jesus highlights another easy way that we can stop trusting Him.

👁 Read Matthew 6 v 25–34

ENGAGE YOUR BRAIN

▶ *If trusting in wealth is one way we can fail to trust God, what's another way we can show our lack of trust? (v25–34)*

▶ *What's the problem with worrying? (v27)*

▶ *How does Jesus reassure His followers? (v26–32)*

▶ *What should our priority be? (v33)*

TALK ABOUT IT

Ever wonder why, if God promises to feed and clothe his children, there are so many Christians in need? Get hold of an older Christian and see if you can work out why that is. (Remember Matt 5 v 10–12 and look up Matt 25 v 41–45 for another suggestion).

▶ *How do you fail to trust God?*

▶ *Do you hedge your bets by trusting in good exam results, getting a good job, relationships etc? And are you always worrying about life?*

Jesus is not saying that life will always be easy — we've already seen that Christians will face hostility and persecution. But He is telling us not to worry. Worry shows a lack of trust in our loving heavenly Father, who cares and is in control, no matter what happens to us.

PRAY ABOUT IT

Jesus says there are only two sorts of ambition. Either you can be self-centred or God-centred. Tell God what yours is. Ask for God's help to trust Him and not to worry.

THE BOTTOM LINE

Seek first God's kingdom and His righteousness.

→ TAKE IT FURTHER

Refresh your memory on page 118.

50 | Plank you very much

We pass judgment (in our heads, if not aloud) on others' hair, clothes, taste in music, behaviour and, if they're Christians, on their lifestyle and Christian "performance". But this isn't what life in God's kingdom should look like.

👁 Read Matthew 7 v 1–6

ENGAGE YOUR BRAIN

▶ What are the dangers of judging others? (v1–2)

▶ How can remembering 5 v 7 and 6 v 14–15 help us to avoid being judgmental?

▶ Why is it stupid to judge our brothers and sisters (AKA other Christians)? (v3–4)

▶ Does v5 suggest we should ignore the speck in our brother's eye (the sin in their life)?

▶ So, how should we deal with helping each other to overcome sin in our lives (v5)?

▶ What and who do you think v6 is talking about?

Ever noticed that the things that annoy you about others are often things which you do yourself? It's much easier to moan about how unreliable X is than to make an effort to keep our promises or arrive on time for stuff. But more than that, when we start judging others and looking down on them, we forget that we deserve God's judgment and are only saved by His mercy.

While being judgmental is something to avoid, there will be times when we need to be discerning — to judge whether something is worth doing or better avoiding. The most precious thing we have is the gospel. Verse 6 is saying that there will be exceptional circumstances when taking Jesus' good news (the pearl) to unbelievers provokes such crazed rejection that we'll have to back off and leave those people in God's hands.

PRAY ABOUT IT

Take a look at Luke 18 v 9–14 and ask God to keep you from being judgmental and self-righteous.

THE BOTTOM LINE

Don't judge or you too will be judged.

→ TAKE IT FURTHER

Walk the plank to page 118.

51 | Knock-on effect

Why do we find it so hard to believe that God is there and that He rewards those who seek Him? Read on for some very famous words.

👁 Read Matthew 7 v 7–11

ENGAGE YOUR BRAIN

▶ What should our attitude be when approaching God? (v7–11)

▶ Why is v8 so reassuring?

▶ But what do we have to do?

▶ What does Jesus remind us about God's character in v11?

Whether it's a request, a worried insistence or long-term searching, such prayers are answered by God. That's the promise. But they'll be answered in God's way, and sometimes that means a loud "No" or "Not yet". Think how rubbish it would be if God answered all your prayers the way you wanted. It would make us so selfish.

PRAY ABOUT IT

Do you find it difficult to pray? Do you think that God is too busy, too disappointed by you sinning yet again, or that your needs are so insignificant that He won't listen to you? Read verses 7–11 again and trust your loving, heavenly Father with your needs and worries.

👁 Read verse 12

▶ How does God want us to treat each other? (v12)

▶ How can you put that into practice today?
At home:

At school/college/work:

Chatting to friends:

THE BOTTOM LINE

Ask and it will be given to you; seek and you will find; knock and the door will be opened to you.

→ TAKE IT FURTHER

Seeking more? Go to page 118.

52 Hit the road

Two gates, two roads, two destinations.
This really is the bottom line.

👁 Read Matthew 7 v 13–14

ENGAGE YOUR BRAIN

▶ Why do you think the gate is wide and the road is easy that leads to destruction?

▶ Why do you think Jesus describes "the road that leads to life" (v14) in the way He does?

▶ Is it hard or easy living as a Christian?

Have you ever caught yourself thinking: "Life would be so much easier if I wasn't a Christian"? Or: "If I wasn't a Christian, I could go to that party / see that film / say what I really think to..."? Yes, the road is easy through the wide gate, but it leads to destruction.

In 1 Corinthians 15 v 19, the apostle Paul says: "If only for this life we have hope in Christ, we are to be pitied more than all men." BUT he goes on to remind us we have an eternal hope

— Jesus was raised from the dead as a guarantee of our future too. The road might be hard now, BUT it leads to life! Perfect life with Jesus.

PRAY ABOUT IT

Ask God to help you live with an eternal perspective, remembering where you are headed when life is tough and remembering that Christ has walked the path first and His Spirit goes with us now.

SHARE IT

Sadly, there are many who take the road to destruction. Can you point out the way to eternal life to a friend or family member today? Jesus is the gate, the way in to eternal life.

THE BOTTOM LINE

Two gates, two roads, two destinations.

⤳ TAKE IT FURTHER

Take the road to page 119.

53 Bad taste

Ever picked a juicy-looking piece of fruit, taken a nice big bite out of it and... YEUCH!!! It tastes disgusting. So bitter. Today Jesus tells us about people who leave a bad taste in the mouth.

👁 **Read Matthew 7 v 15–20**

ENGAGE YOUR BRAIN

▶ *According to these verses, how can we tell if someone is a true follower of Jesus?*

▶ *What is Jesus talking about when He mentions fruit?*

▶ *Why are our actions such a good indication of our hearts?*

▶ *Can you think of a practical example of bad fruit?*

always going to be perfect, but if the fruit is overwhelmingly bad, so is the tree.

▶ *What is the final outcome for these false prophets? (v19)*

▶ *Bearing in mind the first part of chapter 7, how can we be watchful (v15) without becoming judgmental?*

The sort of people Jesus is talking about here — false prophets — are the type of people who have power and influence in the church. Imagine you heard a church leader or youth leader completely denying something in the Bible, or see them stealing money, or find out they're always nasty and sarcastic behind people's backs. Their fruit — their actions — shows the reality of their hearts. Now that's not to say our leaders are

PRAY ABOUT IT

Ask God to help you have a pure heart so that your fruit is good. Ask Him for His help to be watchful and not deceived by false teachers and leaders.

→ **TAKE IT FURTHER**

Pick some more fruit on page 119.

54 | Lord! Lord!

So you talk the talk but do you walk the walk? Are you going to put your money where your mouth is? As James puts it elsewhere in the New Testament, faith without actions is dead.

👁 Read Matthew 7 v 21–23

ENGAGE YOUR BRAIN

▶ What test does Jesus apply to people who claim to follow Him?

▶ What is the evidence these people present to Jesus? (v22)

▶ How do they look as if they are true Christians?

Many people use the right language (the people in v22 call Jesus "Lord") and say the right things. They might look impressive and have high-profile roles in the church (v22) but if they're not doing what God wants, then they're not true disciples.

▶ When does this test take place? (v22)

▶ What is so terrifying about v23?

▶ What does God want us to do? (v21) Clue: John 6 v 29.

On the day of judgment, all our impressive deeds will count for nothing. We can't earn our way into heaven. All we can do is trust in the mercy of God shown in Christ. If Jesus knows us, we are safe.

GET ON WITH IT

Have you done that? Make sure you're not trusting in anything except Jesus.

PRAY ABOUT IT

Pray for anyone you know who's not currently trusting in Jesus. Pray that God would open their eyes and ears to see who Jesus is and to listen to and obey Him.

THE BOTTOM LINE

It's not what you do, it's who you know.

→ TAKE IT FURTHER

A little more on page 119.

55 Firm foundations

As we reach the end of the Sermon on the Mount (well done!), Jesus gives us a stark warning. It's a million miles away from jolly little Sunday-school songs about building your house on the rock too!

👁 Read Acts 7 v 24–29

▷ *What does Jesus want us to do after listening to His teaching (and when we read the Bible generally)? (v24)*

▷ *How can we make sure we do this?*

▷ *Read verses 24–27. What sort of builder are you?*

▷ *What do you think the storm and floods signify?*

You could interpret the storm and floods that the wise and foolish men face as life's trials and difficulties, and it's certainly true that listening to and obeying Jesus is our anchor through tough times. But look back at the previous verses — what was Jesus talking about in verse 22? The ultimate test will come when we all stand before Jesus on the Day of Judgment. Again, Jesus points out

that it is obeying Him — doing what He has told us to do — which will enable us to stand.

▷ *Why is it so important to listen to and obey Jesus? (v29)*

▷ *Do you just talk about being a Christian or do you live it?*

▷ *Don't be downhearted when you fail to be perfect. Remember the beatitudes — what sort of person pleases God? (Matthew 5 v 1–12)*

PRAY ABOUT IT

The most important thing God has told us to do is to listen to His Son (Matthew 17 v 5). Pray now that you would listen to Jesus and obey Him.

THE BOTTOM LINE

Hear Jesus' words and act on them.

→ TAKE IT FURTHER

Final view on page 119.

56 ┆ Down in the pit ┆

Here's a shocker of a psalm — we found it deeply moving. As you read it, please don't just watch this believer's nightmare life. Get inside it and let downbeat parts of the Bible like this speak to you too.

👁 Read Psalm 88 v 1–18

ENGAGE YOUR BRAIN

▶ *What's the psalm writer's mood?*

▶ *What's his situation? (v3–5)*

▶ *So what did he do? (v1, 9, 13)*

▶ *Yet what did he feel had happened? (v6–8, 15–18)*

This guy was in a pit of despair. He remembered nothing but ill health and danger; looking to God, he was terrified; looking for friends, he saw no one at all. The New Testament reminds God's people to expect suffering before glory. That's what happened to Jesus and it's the same for all Christians.

▶ *What's commendable about this suffering believer? (v1, 9, 13)*

He held on in faith to God even in disaster and in total confusion. Day and night he completed his prayer, in the dark and totally unrewarded. And he kept going. But he was prepared to leave all matters — of life and death and all he couldn't understand — in God's hands.

THINK IT OVER

▶ *What truths about God can you hold on to when life seems hopeless?*

▶ *What's the best way to help friends in such a situation?*

PRAY ABOUT IT

Talk to God about whatever's on your heart and pray for people who seem to be in the depths of despair.

→ TAKE IT FURTHER

Hope for the hopeless on page 119.

57

Shout it out!

Psalm 89 is a giant, so we'll look at it over two days. On the way we'll learn loads about God's greatness, His power and His character. Let's dive straight in.

👁 Read Psalm 89 v 1–8

ENGAGE YOUR BRAIN

▷ What two things was this psalmist shouting about? (v1–2)

▷ How exactly had God shown these qualities? (v3–4)

▷ What does the writer conclude about God? (v8)

We know from the Bible that God has made great promises, like His covenant with David (v3). But things happen to us that make us think God's dropped His promises and walked out on His people. But our God is faithful. We can look at how He kept all His promises in the Bible. We can look to the skies and see how great He is, shown in all He's created.

👁 Read verses 9–18

▷ What are we told about God's power? (v9–11)

▷ How does the writer describe God's character? (v14)

▷ So how should we respond to this God? (v15)

▷ How else? (v16)

▷ Why? (v17)

GET ON WITH IT

▷ How is your idea of God sometimes wrong?

▷ How should you respond to the God described in this psalm?

▷ What exactly do you need to change?

PRAY ABOUT IT

Use verses 1–2 and 14–16 to influence the way you pray today.

→ TAKE IT FURTHER

Grab some more on page 120.

58 | Promising prayer

Yesterday, the psalm writer gave us great reasons to trust God's promises and shout about His love and faithfulness. Now he focuses on God's covenant with His people and how they'd treated Him.

Read Psalm 89 v 19–29

ENGAGE YOUR BRAIN

▣ *What did God promise David?*
  v21–23:

  v24–25:

  v27:

  v28:

  v29:

Read verses 30–37

▣ *What would happen if David or his descendants failed to obey God? (v32)*

▣ *What wouldn't happen? (v33)*

▣ *Why not? (v34–37)*

Read verses 38–45

▣ *Had God really renounced / given up on the covenant? (v39) (Find the answer in 2 Corinthians 1 v 20)*

Read verses 46–52

▣ *What did he call on God to do? (v49–51)*

▣ *Yet how did he finish the psalm?*

God had promised to establish David's line (v1–37) but spot the disaster God hit Israel's king with (v38–45). This was actually v30–32 coming true for Israel's king. But v33–37 could also be true because God would send King Jesus.

PRAY ABOUT IT

Get the point for us? When events in our lives make us question God's love and faithfulness, take God's promises, pray about them and trust them. Try it right now.

→ TAKE IT FURTHER

No *Take it further* today.

Sanctification

In *Essential*, we take time out to explore key truths about God, the Bible and Christianity. This issue we ask: Sanctification — what does it mean and why's it so important?

MAKING CHANGES

Do you ever feel that you're not quite the person you're designed to be? Ever wish you could change? Become better at controlling what comes out of your mouth? Get rid of some irritating habit? Trust God more?

Well, good news! God is unchanging. But He is passionate about encouraging His children to change. He loves to help people who follow Jesus to become more like Jesus. And it all happens through a process called "sanctification".

It's important to remember that God doesn't change us to make us acceptable to Him. He treasures us just as we are — no matter how messed up. But He loves us too much to leave us as we are. And He's keen to mould us into people who reflect Jesus Christ. This work of change is:

GOD'S WORK

The moment we become a Christian, God gives us His Spirit (Ephesians 1 v 13). He lives inside us and gradually changes our hearts and minds in ways that we might not always notice. He helps us to remember how great Jesus is and how complete our forgiveness is (John 16 v 5–15). He helps us to be faithful to our decision to follow Jesus by increasing our patience, gentleness, goodness and self-control (Galatians 5 v 22–23). God is infinitely wise, so we can be confident that any changes He makes are good for us. And God is powerful, so we can be sure there's no mess in our lives that He can't turn around.

OUR WORK

But it's not a case of just sitting back and letting God do His work while we do nothing (Galatians 5 v 25). The Bible tells us that we need to make every effort to change too (2 Peter 1 v 5–7). God wants us to exercise self-control (Titus 2 v 11–12) and make the effort to stay away from things that tempt us to stop following Jesus closely (2 Corinthians 6 v 14). He wants you to be *"transformed by the renewing of your mind"* (Romans 12 v 2), which means deliberately changing so you think, say and do things God's way — and you can do that by:

- reading the Bible (Psalm 119 v 9–11)
- being really involved in a church where you can give and receive encouragement (Hebrews 10 v 24–25)
- praying (Philippians 4 v 6)

A LIFETIME'S WORK

The Christian life is a lifetime of change. Step by step we become more like Jesus. Sometimes the change will be quick — at other times it will take years, even decades, to turn around some sin that we struggle with. And we will never reach perfection in this life. We'll never get to the point where we stop messing up and needing God's forgiveness… not until Jesus comes back anyway. But when Jesus does return, we'll be totally transformed (1 Corinthians 13 v 10) and we'll be completely perfect, forever! (1 Corinthians 15 v 49)

EXCITING WORK

All in all sanctification is really exciting! As God works in us, and we make every effort to follow Him, we change in amazing ways. Bit by bit we discover that the things we once struggled with melt away. Gradually we find it a little easier to react in the ways God would like, to put God first in everything we do — in the good times and the bad. That's great for us. It pleases our heavenly Father. And as the people around us see us change, they may want to know how and why the change is happening, which gives us a great opportunity to tell them about Jesus — which is fantastic for them too (Philippians 2 v 14–16)!

So why not take a moment now to pray and talk to God about the changes He wants to make in your life?

59 Revelation: Revealing Jesus

Time to rejoin Revelation and the third series of events describing history between Jesus' resurrection and return. We've been shown tyranny (chs. 6–7) and chaos (chs. 8–11). Next up is persecution (chs. 12–14).

◉ Read Revelation 12 v 1–6

ENGAGE YOUR BRAIN
▷ *What did John see next? (v1–2)*

▷ *What terrifying thing happened? (v3–4)*

▷ *How was the dragon foiled? (v5–6)*

The woman represents God's people and she's about to give birth to Jesus. The dragon stands for Satan. All his heads, horns and crowns stand for power and authority. He was hoping to destroy Christ (v4) but his plan failed: Jesus was born and was taken up to heaven (after His death and resurrection) where He rules with God (v5). In the meantime, God's people are in the desert (v6) — God is caring for them on earth before they go to live with HIm in heaven.

◉ Read verses 7–12
▷ *What happened to the devil and his angels? (v7–9)*

▷ *What is Satan's aim? (v9)*

▷ *Who defeated Satan? (v10–11)*

Jesus has already defeated Satan! And Christians share in that victory. We overcome the devil by relying on and talking about Jesus' victory at the cross. The bad news is that Satan is furious and is currently taking out his anger on Christians. But his time won't last for long (v12).

◉ Read verses 13–17
Satan is out to get the church — all believers. But he won't succeed because God protects them. The devil will attack us, but if we choose to live God's way, He'll always give us a way to escape.

PRAY ABOUT IT
Thank God that He's already defeated Satan and that He protects Christians.

→ TAKE IT FURTHER
More revelations on page 120.

60 Simply the beast

Satan's aim is to lead the whole world away from God. He does this using political powers and false prophets. Of course, Revelation paints a wilder, more dramatic picture of this with sea beasts and giant monsters!

Read Revelation 13 v 1–10

ENGAGE YOUR BRAIN

- Where does the beast get his power? (v2)

- What does this beast do? (v6–7)

- How does the world react to the beast? (v3–4)

This sea beast seems to symbolise political regimes which Satan (the dragon) uses to oppress God's people and demand worship from the world. In many nations, political and religious powers speak against Christianity and throw Christians into prison. But these powers won't last forever.

Read verses 11–18

- What does the second beast do? (v11–12)

- How does he deceive people? (v13–14)

- What happens to people under this beast's authority? (v15–17)

This beast is false religion. It looks like Jesus (the lamb) but speaks for the dragon, Satan (v11). It performs miracles too. But we can see through such fake leaders — if their message is not the gospel of Jesus, the rest is irrelevant however impressive it looks.

When false religion is backed by corrupt political power, Christians suffer (v15). This happens all over the world. Sometimes there will be violent persecution. Quite often though it's simply the loss of economic and social privileges (v17). Christians can't get jobs or miss out on promotion for sticking to their principles.

PRAY ABOUT IT

Pray for Christians you know who are persecuted for their faith. Research two countries where Christians are persecuted. Pray for them regularly.

→ TAKE IT FURTHER

What's 666 mean? Page 120.

61

Angelic messages

We've been warned that the beast is at work. Next, Revelation talks about the church during this time and about the devastating final judgment which will bring the end for God's enemies.

Read Revelation 14 v 1–5

ENGAGE YOUR BRAIN

▶ *What do you think this is all about?*

Back in chapter 7, we learned that this 144,000 stands for all of God's people (and there are actually millions of them). Here they are, safe with Jesus ("the Lamb"). Christians will get a tough time on earth but they can be certain of eternity with Christ. Believers try to stay sexually pure, avoid lies and follow Jesus.

Read verses 6–13

▶ *What's angel 1's message and who is it for? (v6)*

▶ *What's the right response? (v7)*

▶ *What does angel 2 say is the future for Babylon — those who reject God? (v8)*

▶ *Angel 3: What will happen to Satan's followers? (v9–11)*

▶ *What's required of Christians (saints) until Jesus returns? (v12)*

Before the victory is complete, believers have the task of spreading the gospel (the message of the angels). We want people to avoid God's punishment and give Him glory instead. So we've got to tell them about Jesus.

SHARE IT

Spend time thinking how you can share the gospel effectively with the people you most often come into contact with.

PRAY ABOUT IT

Thank God that His people are safe and have a great future ahead of them. Ask Him to help you share the gospel even when it's difficult.

→ TAKE IT FURTHER

More messages on page 120.

62   Grim reaping

And now for a straightforward and boring part
of Revelation. Not really — time for more angels,
a devastating harvest, some plagues and some
great singing.

Read Revelation 14 v 14–20

ENGAGE YOUR BRAIN

Who's in charge? (v14)

What was it time for? (v15)

What terrible image is used for
the fate of those who worship the
beast? (v19–20)

Jesus will return as Judge. At this final
harvest, those who've trusted Jesus
for rescue and forgiveness will be
gathered to Him. But those who've
rejected Him and ignored God's
warnings will be punished.

Read Revelation 15 v 1–4

What did these angels have with
them? (v1)

Who else was present? (v2)

What were they doing? (v3)

What aspects of God's character
did they sing about? (v3–4)

So how should everyone respond?
(v4)

In Moses' time, God's people
sang about the Lord defeating the
Egyptians and rescuing His people.
When Jesus returns, His people will
sing His praises for defeating sin and
death and the devil. And for rescuing
them, bring them to eternal safety.

More on the angels with plagues
coming tomorrow.

PRAY ABOUT IT
Plead with God to rescue friends
who are heading for His punishment.
Then praise Him, using 15 v 3–4 to
focus on His perfect holiness.

THE BOTTOM LINE
God alone is holy. All nations will
worship Him.

→ TAKE IT FURTHER
Check out what Jesus said about
sowing and reaping. Page 121.

63 Angels of destruction

It's time for the last of the four series of events which describe history between Jesus' resurrection and return. This time the focus is on destruction and God's final judgment.

👁 Read Rev 15 v 5 – 16 v 7

▶ What did these angels bring? (15 v 7)

▶ Who gets the full blast of God's anger? (16 v 2)

▶ What happens to the sea? (v3–4)

▶ Why is this fair? (v5–7)

The main targets of God's fair punishment are those who rejected Jesus and so are on the beast's (Satan's) side. The sea is turned to blood and everything in it dies. This is punishing those who have shed the blood of believers.

👁 Read Revelation 16 v 8–16

▶ What other punishment is dished out? (v8, 10, 12)

▶ What two responses did people have? (v9, v11)

Surely people would turn to God and repent. Well, some people do turn to God when faced with suffering. But many curse God and refuse to admit their sin and their need for God. (For the lowdown on v13–16, go to *Take it further*).

👁 Read verses 17–21

▶ What was the effect of this final "plague"? (v19–21)

Instead of describing the final battle hinted at in v13–16, the scene switches to the final judgment. It's horrific and yet people are still unrepentant and cursing God (v21). And there's more to come, but we'll read about that tomorrow.

PRAY ABOUT IT

Remember people you care about who refuse to listen to God or trust Jesus. Spend longer than usual praying for each of them, that they would admit their sin and turn to Jesus for forgiveness.

➔ TAKE IT FURTHER

Follow the frogs to page 121.

64 Toxic temptation

The message of Revelation 17 is BEWARE! Be very, very ware. The godless lifestyle of this world can be very seductive... but it doesn't deliver what it offers and has a limited future.

Read Revelation 17 v 1–6

ENGAGE YOUR BRAIN
- *What impact did the prostitute have on the world? (v2)*
- *And on God's people? (v6)*

The prostitute in John's vision represents godless society through the ages — from ancient Babylon and Rome to everywhere and everyone who seduce people away from God with hideous sin (v4). And everyone who persecutes God's people (v6)

Read verses 7–14
- *How is the beast described and how will he affect the world? (v8)*
- *What's his attitude towards Jesus? (v14)*
- *Who will win and why? (v14)*

We've met this beast before — he represents cruel rulers. Non-Christians especially are impressed by such powerful leaders (v8). But such evil powers will be destroyed by Jesus (v14). (V9–14 covered on p121.)

Read verses 15–18
- *What's surprising about the prostitute's downfall? (v16)*
- *Who is really in control? (v17)*

The devil's at work behind the godless regimes of this world. But in the end, they self-destruct because God's in control (v17). Chapter 17 shows us the attraction of living life without God. It's tempting, oh so seductive, and so liberating, we think. But a life of materialism or self-serving pleasure contains its own self-destruct button. It won't satisfy or deliver... and it won't give any hope for the future beyond death.

PRAY ABOUT IT
Talk to God honestly about the things that seduce and tempt you away from Him. Thank Him that Jesus is the winner, not the devil. And ask Him to help you choose the winning side and live accordingly.

→ TAKE IT FURTHER
Tempting offer on page 121.

65 | Babylon bashed

Godless society ("Babylon") has its attractions. Revelation shows it up for what it really is: short-lived and under God's judgment. Before launching His new world (ch 21–22), God destroys all evil in His final judgment (ch 18–20).

👁 Read Revelation 18 v 1–8

ENGAGE YOUR BRAIN

▷ *How is Babylon described? (v2–3)*

▷ *Why must God's people keep away from Babylon? (v4)*

▷ *What will happen to Babylon? (v8)*

There are so many temptations in the world — sex and wealth (v3) are two of the biggest ones. It's easy to think that, as Christians, we're immune to these temptations without noticing they're already seducing us.

👁 Read verses 9–24

▷ *How will rulers react to Babylon's downfall? (v9)*

▷ *What about salesmen? (v15–16)*

▷ *But what about believers? (v20)*

▷ *Why will Babylon be destroyed? (v23–24)*

Babylon stands for life without God. Despite all the warnings, many people would rather live for themselves and ignore God completely. Wealth and greed in particular pull people away from God. So many people chase after the "good life" rather than a God life. But Babylon will be destroyed and God's people will celebrate.

GET ON WITH IT

▷ *In what ways are you greedy?*

▷ *How do sex or relationships pull you away from God?*

▷ *What temptations do you need to deal with right now?*

PRAY ABOUT IT

Ask God's help to fight the specific temptations you struggle with. Pray, too, for friends who are being pulled away from God by the world.

→ TAKE IT FURTHER

Babble on... page 121.

66 White wedding

Yesterday we read about Babylon's downfall.
Godless living ultimately ends in destruction.
Today we're invited to a wedding party.
I bet you can't guess who's getting married.

👁 **Read Revelation 19 v 1–5**

ENGAGE YOUR BRAIN

▷ Why is life with God better than life without Him ("Babylon")? (v1–2)

▷ What's the response once God's enemies have been defeated? (v5)

It's not popular to talk about God's judgment. But we must remember that any punishment from God is totally fair. In fact, God's judgment is a cause for celebration. We can praise and thank God for being true and fair and punishing evil as well as rescuing His people.

👁 **Read verses 6–10**

▷ What else was worth celebrating? (v7)

▷ Who's getting hitched?

▷ Why was John wrong to worship the angel? (v10)

All heaven celebrates as God's enemies are defeated and God's kingdom is established. Time for a wedding! Jesus (the Lamb) is getting married. But who could possibly be married to Jesus? Well, the rest of the Bible says that the church — God's people — are His bride. Amazing. Believers will be with Christ for ever.

The chapter ends on a strange note with John being told off for worshipping the angel messenger. Only God deserves our worship and devotion. Angels are God's servants just as we are. It's the message of Christ and what He's done for us that matters, not the messenger. So don't be tempted to idolise people who teach you. Save hero worship for God.

PRAY ABOUT IT AGAIN

Use today's verses to help you praise God in prayer right now.

➔ **TAKE IT FURTHER**

More married bliss on page 122.

79

67 | Conquering King

At the final judgment, God will destroy all who oppose Him. In a great end-time battle? No, that's already happened. Jesus has won already, on the cross. Now it's time to finish off those enemies...

👁 Read Revelation 19 v 11–16

ENGAGE YOUR BRAIN

▶ How is this terrifying figure described?
v11:
v12:
v13:
▶ What has He come to do? (v15)
▶ Who is He? (v16)

This is Jesus — and He's not to be messed with. The blood on His robes (v13) probably refers to His death, which brought victory over His enemies (v15). The sharp sword that comes out of His mouth is the word of God and its effect is devastating. There is no doubt who the winner is — Jesus is King of kings and Lord of lords (v16). He is God and He's boss of everything.

👁 Read verses 17–21

▶ What does the devil (and all who reject God) do? (v19)
▶ How do you see that attitude in people around you?

▶ What happens to those who rebel against God? (v20–21)

Yesterday we read about the great wedding feast for all believers. Here, the birds are invited to feast on the bodies of God's defeated enemies (v17–18). Grim. They all think they can defeat God but the battle is over immediately. The beast and false prophet are captured and destroyed. The rest of the evil armies are defeated by God's word (v21).

THINK IT OVER
This is a terrible picture of what happens to those who reject God. We all need to take in the reality of this.

▶ What motivation is there here for us to tell others about this?
▶ How does Jesus in v11–16 differ from the usual view of Him?
▶ How might your thinking about Jesus need to change?

➔ TAKE IT FURTHER
A little bit more on page 122.

68 | Satan's doom

The judgment goes on: it's Satan himself who's now in trouble. Then everybody faces God's judgment. Yes, everybody. What's described next is the final judgment and the time leading up to it.

👁 **Read Revelation 20 v 1–6**

ENGAGE YOUR BRAIN

▶ *What happens to Satan? (v1–3)*
▶ *Who share in Jesus' victory at this time? (v4)*

Christians often argue over when this "1000 year" reign will take place. We'll look more in-depth at it in *Take it further*. During this time, the devil will be thrown into a bottomless pit (v1) and stopped from deceiving the nations (v3). This isn't the final judgment as Satan will be released again for a short time. The suggestion is that during this "1000 years" Satan's influence will be restricted by the faithfulness of Christians, many prepared to die for the gospel (v4–6).

👁 **Read verses 7–10**

▶ *What will Satan do when he's released? (v8)*
▶ *But what would happen to the devil and his army? (v10)*

Satan is released for a limited time and will gather God's enemies from all the nations. But this mighty-looking rebellion ends as soon as it's begun and the devil will be punished for ever. Notice that Satan suffers the same punishment as all who reject God — he won't be enjoying hell!

👁 **Read verses 11–15**

▶ *Who will face the final judgment? & how will they be judged? (v12)*
▶ *Who will be punished? (v15)*

The enemies of God have been destroyed; now everyone who has ever lived will be judged. No one can avoid it and they'll be judged on what they've done in their lives. Everyone who has trusted in Jesus to save them will be OK. But those who've ignored or dismissed God will be punished.

PRAY ABOUT IT

Thank God for Jesus' victory and the fact all believers share in it. Now pray for 3 more people you know who refuse to trust in Jesus.

➔ **TAKE IT FURTHER**

1000 years of stuff on page 122.

69 | The future's bright

Satan is defeated and all God's enemies have been punished. So what will happen to believers and where will they live? It's time for "Jerusalem II — The Comeback".

👁 Read Revelation 21 v 1–4

ENGAGE YOUR BRAIN

▷ *What did John see next? (v1–2)*

▷ *What is the amazing news for God's people? (v3)*

▷ *What will never happen again? (v4)*

The Bible doesn't actually tell us much about eternal life. But what it does tell us is tantalising. Most importantly, God will live with His people — in fact He'll bring heaven down to us! (v2) Heaven and earth will be united: the original relationship between God and humans which existed in the Garden of Eden will be restored. There will be no more sadness or suffering.

👁 Read verses 5–8

▷ *How does God describe Himself? (v6)*

▷ *What will He give to believers?*
v6:
v7:

▷ *What about everyone else? (v8)*

The message for us is: "Keep going!" If we stick at it ("endure") and keep trusting in Jesus, the future is so bright! The alternative is horrific (v8).

PRAY ABOUT IT

Go through today's reading, verse by verse, using it to prompt your prayers.

THE BOTTOM LINE

"Now the dwelling of God is with men, and he will live with them. They will be his people, and God himself will be with them and be their God."

→ TAKE IT FURTHER

Another look into the future on page 123.

70 Bright lights, big city

No tears, no pain, no death. Revelation ends, as it began, with a vision. It's a vision of the new creation, a reality which helps us make sense of all that we experience here and now.

Read Revelation 21 v 9–22

ENGAGE YOUR BRAIN

- ▶ *What was the angel going to show John? (v9)*
- ▶ *What did John actually see? (v10)*
- ▶ *What was it like? (v11–21)*
- ▶ *Why was there no temple — a place to worship God? (v22)*

It will be glorious and brilliant. Literally. The bride and the city are pictures of God's people, who will be with Him when He fulfils His promises. The twelve tribes (v12) and twelve apostles (v14) represent the whole of God's people. They'll all be there.

In the Old Testament, the temple symbolised God's presence. In the new Jerusalem there won't be a need for a temple because God will actually live with His people there.

Read verses 23–27

- ▶ *Why no sun or moon? (v23)*
- ▶ *What will fill God's city? (v24–26)*
- ▶ *What will not be there? (v27)*
- ▶ *Who will be there? (v27)*

Read Revelation 22 v 1–5

We've seen that the city is the source of the world's light. Here, the river flowing from it shows us it's also the source of life. The tree of life (last seen in the Garden of Eden in Genesis) is in God's new city to bring healing to people of all nations. There will be no more suffering. God will now live with His people in His perfect city. Incredible.

PRAY ABOUT IT

Thank God that His people will live in a new, perfect place, better than Eden; they'll have a face-to-face relationship with Him that can never be spoiled.

THE BOTTOM LINE

The future is perfect for God's people.

→ TAKE IT FURTHER

Follow the bright lights to page 123.

71 | The last word

Time to look back. Jesus is at the centre of John's vision and He's won a great victory for His people. So remember: whatever difficulties and opposition you face, Christians are on the winning side. Hang in there.

👁 Read Revelation 22 v 6–11

ENGAGE YOUR BRAIN

- ▶ *What does Jesus remind us of? (v7)*
- ▶ *When is the message of Revelation for? (v10)*
- ▶ *So what's happening right now? (v11)*

Revelation is a letter from John and it ends with loads of short bits of info and instruction. Believers should act on what they've heard in Revelation (v7). We must worship only God (v8–9). Jesus reminds us that the book is for now, not just the future (v10), yet life will continue as normal (v11).

👁 Read verses 12–16

- ▶ *How does Jesus describe Himself? (v13, 16)*
- ▶ *How would you put v14 in your own words?*
- ▶ *And v15?*

All the names that Jesus gives Himself here remind us that He is God. One day (possibly soon) He will return and everyone who trusts in Him will be rewarded. But everyone else will be thrown out of God's presence.

👁 Read verses 17–21

- ▶ *Who's inviting who to what? (v17)*
- ▶ *What's the final warning? (v18–19)*
- ▶ *What should be our attitude after reading Revelation? (v20)*

We've all been invited to take the free gift of eternal life made available through Jesus' death. So life may be tough for Christians, but we should be looking forward to a perfect future with Him.

PRAY ABOUT IT

Having read this incredible book, only you know what you need to talk to God about.

→ TAKE IT FURTHER

One last revelation on page 123.

Obadiah

Tables turned

Welcome to the 6th century BC. Obadiah is one of the shortest books in the Bible, so let's not hang around. It's time to meet the major players.

EDOM

This nation thought they were unbeatable. They lived in a mountainous place called Edom, south-east of Israel. This bunch of people were descended from Esau, the twin of Jacob — sons of Isaac and grandsons of Abraham. The Edomites were a pain in the neck for centuries to the people of Judah (God's people, descended from Jacob). Edom always attacked them and never helped them out. Most recently, they had not only refused to help out when Jerusalem was invaded — they stood by and watched it get trashed. And gloated.

JUDAH

Let's cheer for God's team! Actually, there wasn't much to be cheerful about. The people God chose were mostly rubbish at living for Him, despite all His care. They couldn't be bothered to worship Him properly or do what He said or trust Him. So, rightly, God punished His people. He sent the Babylonian army into Jerusalem to take His people away as captives. Maybe in Babylon, miles from home, they'd turn to Him again.

OBADIAH

Obadiah was one of God's mob. As a prophet, his job was to speak God's words. His message was this: God would punish Edom (who'd arrogantly shown no respect for God or His people) and bring God's suffering people back home. What a promise! But there was no room for gloating about Edom. God said one day He'd punish all nations. And He meant it.

Obadiah tells us that God does judge, and God does rescue. Too often we forget one or the other, or ignore them both. So let God speak through Obadiah, and make sure you listen carefully.

72 | Pride before a fall

God's mob, Judah, had been punished by Him — dragged off into exile — and they knew they deserved that. But how could God let Edom join in the ransacking of Jerusalem? Didn't Edom deserve punishment too?

👁 Read verses 1–7

ENGAGE YOUR BRAIN

▶ What was God's message for Edom? (v1–2)

▶ Why? (v3)

▶ How thorough would God's punishment be? (v5–6)

▶ What would Edom's friends and allies do? (v7)

God didn't remain silent — He spoke through His messenger Obadiah. God's people in Judah could be sure that the Lord would punish their enemies. Edom had built their cities in mountain areas and thought they were safe and powerful. But God would bring them down (v4). They couldn't even turn to their friends — Edom's allies would be the ones attacking them!

The danger in feeling secure and successful is that you think things will never change, and you're responsible for how good life is. The message Obadiah brought to God's people was intended to comfort them — God would judge the Edomites for their pride. But it was a reminder to them not to get arrogant too.

In Jesus' death, God showed His judgment on sin. His final judgment, sorting out all wrong, is still to come. So, Christians must keep going till then, trusting Jesus. And not get proud: God's not interested in those who think they can offer Him something, but in those who know they must rely on Him to rescue them.

THINK IT THROUGH

▶ How are you proud?

▶ How do you rely on your own abilities rather than on God?

▶ What will you do about it?

→ TAKE IT FURTHER
Jacob and Esau are on page 123.

73 | Relative trouble

Facing opposition for being a Christian isn't easy.
When it comes from friends or family it can become
unbearable. God's mob, the Judeans, had turned their
backs on God and had been punished for it.

But it was their relatives the Edomites who'd helped the Babylonians storm Jerusalem. So was God now on the side of nations who opposed His own people? Obadiah tells the people exactly what he thinks:

Read verses 8–14

ENGAGE YOUR BRAIN
- What was God's plan for Edom? (v8–9)

- Why? (v10)

- What exactly had they done to God's people?
  v11:
  v12:
  v13:
  v14:

Way back, God chose Jacob to be the father of the Israelite people. Edom had always refused to accept this. Time and time again, they caused trouble with God's people. But this latest incident was the worst yet. Edom had acted like an enemy, not a brother. God's threats were not empty. Several years later, Edom was destroyed.

THINK IT OVER
- Who have you been violent towards recently (vicious words and thoughts count too)?

- Who have you failed to stand up for?

- Who do you look down on?

- Who do you take advantage of?

- Ever happy about someone else's downfall?

PRAY ABOUT IT
Talk over your answers with God, saying sorry and asking His help in putting things right.

→ TAKE IT FURTHER
More on page 124.

74 | Mountain rescue

It's said the hardest person to forgive is yourself. We can forgive friends most of the time. But when we've really messed things up ourselves, we often don't believe we can be forgiven.

Well, God's people (now in captivity or scattered all over the place) knew they'd deserved God's punishment. Some of them now thought this was the end of their relationship with God. Was it?

👁 Read verses 15–21

ENGAGE YOUR BRAIN

▶ How is God's punishment of Edom a warning for everyone? (v15)
▶ But what was the promise for God's people? (v17–21)

The Edomites drank to celebrate Jerusalem's destruction. In fact, all of the nations would be drinking (v16). Not in celebration — they'd be drinking a huge measure of God's punishment. In His final judgment, God will punish everyone who opposes Him and His people.

There was hope for God's people. They wouldn't be wiped out and they'd return to Jerusalem (Mount Zion). Those who tried to annihilate them would be destroyed.

God promised rescue for His people: that's true for us too. God must judge us for our sins, but the great news is He's already taken the punishment on Himself. We can escape His judgment when we trust Jesus' death to rescue us for eternal life.

That's why being a Christian is remarkable. God's seen you at your worst — and has still sent His Son to die for you. The God we run to for forgiveness is the judge of the world. The one before who we stand guilty is the one who has rescued us.

PRAY ABOUT IT

What an incredible God, don't you think? Why not tell Him? And thank God that He loves you to such an extent that He punished Jesus instead of you.

→ TAKE IT FURTHER

Emergency services on page 124.

75 | Food fright

Ready for a psalm psandwich? The bread on the outside (v1, v12–17) tastes good — it's all about a relationship with God. But the filling (v2–11) is harder to swallow — tough truths about God and us.

👁 Read Psalm 90 v 1–6

ENGAGE YOUR BRAIN

▶ Where can God's people find safety? (v1)

▶ What does v2 tell us about God?

▶ How do humans differ from God? (v3–6)

Our lives are brief (v4), fragile (v5), quickly over (v5–6), and we're at God's disposal (v3) But what's brought God's curse on us?

👁 Read verses 7–12

▶ What is terrifying about God? (v7, 9, 11)

▶ What is God angry about? (v8)

▶ How do many people view this life? (v10)

▶ But what should be our prayer? (v12)

👁 Read verses 13–17

▶ What can life be like for God's people? (v14–15)

▶ What should give us joy? (v16)

▶ What else should we pray? (v17)

God's people today (Christians) live after Jesus has come — the cross has shown God's compassion and unfailing love (v13–14). Jesus brought His people peace with God — a rescue from God's wrath (anger and punishment). Doesn't that give joy to life now?

PRAY ABOUT IT

So thank God for what this psalm's taught you. And make v14 your prayer too.

→ TAKE IT FURTHER

No *Take it further* today.

French connection

Kevin Mosi Da Costa is a 20-year-old Christian from Paris. Kevin isn't a very French name, but his mum was a big fan of the actor Kevin Costner. *Engage* caught up with him to ask what it's like being a young Christian in France.

Are there lots of Christians in France?

Yes, there are a lot of Christians in France but it's hard to recognise each other outside the church or youth meetings. It feels as if outside the church everybody is non-Christian and you can quickly feel pretty alone. I think this is due to the separation between the church and the state in France.

People don't really talk about religious stuff in public. You can be whatever you want in private but in the public you are just a citizen like everyone else. Consequently there must be no apparent distinction between you and anyone else.

How does this make life difficult for Christians?

So, for instance, this principle prevents a teacher from talking about God or being seen with a Bible in school. It prevents a student from wearing any religious sign (like a cross) in an obvious way. The principle applies also at workplaces, public places such as parks, restaurants, any official building, on TV or radio and even in the street.

In fact, reading your Bible on the train or the bus is not only seen as inappropriate but for some people it is breaking the law. For many French people (mainly non-believers) this principle is the cornerstone of our social and political unity. So any act which goes against it is morally condemned. Public opinion considers that

we have Sunday mornings to do our "religious things" so during the week we should stay quiet.

What is the hardest thing about being a Christian in Paris?

It's really hard being a Christian! The moment you start talking about God or even opening your Bible, you are seen as a proselytizer (someone who "forces" their faith on others). It's hard to live a Christian life outside the walls of your home or church. We feel that we're under a *"Don't ask, don't tell"* policy when it comes to Jesus.

How has God helped you to grow in your faith?

God encouraged me by making me realise how large the Christian family is and that I am not alone. He encouraged me also through the life of other Christians. To see God making them grow in their faith and changing them to be more like Him, it is just a miracle!

How has getting to know Christians outside of France helped you?

The encouragement of getting to know Christians abroad is indescribable. My main experience was at a Christian summer camp in the UK. It is both encouraging to see other brothers and sisters persevere in Christ, and heart-warming to see that you are not alone and that other Christian are struggling alongside you for the glory of the Lord.

I think the most encouraging thing is to see how huge the family of God is and how good it is to be together to glorify our Maker. It was like a preview of heaven! Words fail me to express it but if you have the opportunity to visit other Christians abroad, just do it and you will know what I am talking about!

What would you like people to pray for France and Christian students there?

For us to be and to stay genuine followers of Christ. To be faithful to Him even if it seems impossible to be so. To not let the world rule our lives but let Jesus be our guide to convince the world that He is the way, the truth and the life.

76 | 2 Samuel: Kingdom come

Today we return to the saga of King David and his disfunctional family. Remember Bathsheba? David had committed adultery and murder. Well, like father, like sons...

👁 Read 2 Samuel 13 v 1–6

ENGAGE YOUR BRAIN

- ▷ *What was Amnon's problem? (v1–2)*
- ▷ *What was Jonadab's plan? (v5)*

Amnon was David's eldest son and heir to the throne. Tamar was his half-sister so he couldn't marry her or even get near her. He should have left it at that, but lust and temptation can be powerful enemies.

👁 Read verses 7–22

- ▷ *What reasons did Tamar give for not having sex? (v12–13)*
- ▷ *But what happened? (v14–16)*
- ▷ *Did David do anything about it? (v21)*

👁 Read verses 23–39

- ▷ *What action did Absalom take?*
- ▷ *What did that lead to? (v38)*
- ▷ *How did David react? (v36, v39)*

Does Absalom's skill at arranging a death remind you of anyone? For Absalom, the death was a double plus: revenge would be sweet and it would make him heir to the throne. This all led to deadlock — David refused to punish Absalom and longed to see him. But Ab' didn't dare return home. Not yet anyway.

Two reminders lurk in these grubby events:
1. What God says, happens.
2. Sin has consequences.
From now on in 2 Samuel it gets worse. David's great kingdom is becoming a mess. So it points us ahead — God's huge promises (chapter 7) would be fulfilled in a greater son of David: Jesus.

PRAY ABOUT IT

Talk to God about any temptations you're struggling with or any revenge on your mind. Ask God to help you remain faithful to Him.

→ TAKE IT FURTHER

More about David's dynasty on p124.

77 Absalom's return

David had committed murder and adultery. God
had promised: "Out of your own household I am going
to bring calamity upon you." Over the next few
chapters, we'll see this happening again and again.

👁 **Read 2 Samuel 14 v 1–22**

ENGAGE YOUR BRAIN

ⓘ *What did Joab do? (v2–3)*

ⓘ *Why? (v1)*

ⓘ *What was the real message for
David? (v13–14)*

ⓘ *What did David realise? (v19)*

ⓘ *What did David do? (v21)*

👁 **Read verses 23–33**

ⓘ *What restrictions were placed on
Absalom's return? (v24)*

ⓘ *Why are we told about his hair?
(The answer's in chapter 18.)*

ⓘ *Who was still on Absalom's mind?
(v27)*

ⓘ *Who else was on his mind?
(v28–29)*

ⓘ *What did he do to get attention?
(v30–32)*

ⓘ *What was the result? (v35)*

Comeback of the year. Absalom had
vengefully murdered his brother
and lived in exile as a result. Army
commander Joab arranged for
Absalom's return. But David would
have nothing to do with him. A risky
move by Ab (v32) led to him being
back in the king's favour. And with
Amnon dead, Absalom was now heir
to David's throne. The family calamity
will continue. Watch this space.

PRAY ABOUT IT

Take this opportunity to pray for
your family. Particularly think of any
difficult circumstances or relatives
who don't talk to each other. Often
it's not obvious why certain things
happen. But pray that God will make
things work out for His glory.

→ **TAKE IT FURTHER**

No *Take it further* today.

78 | Son rise

Murderer Absalom has returned to Jerusalem.
But it's not enough for him that his father David
has taken him back. He wants David's throne for himself.

👁 Read 2 Samuel 15 v 1–12

ENGAGE YOUR BRAIN

▶ How did Absalom try to gain
popularity? (v1–5)

▶ How well did it work? (v6, 12)

Even David's top adviser, Ahithophel,
turned against the king and joined
Absalom's side.

👁 Read verses 13–23

▶ What was the bad news for
David? (v13)

▶ What was his response? (v14)

▶ Why did David try to send Ittai
away? (v19–20)

▶ What was Ittai's brilliant reply?
(v21)

▶ What did the people do when
they saw their king leaving? (v23)

David got the message and left
Jerusalem. A battle was brewing.
Surely David's little posse out in the
hill country would be no match for
Ab's big numbers? But David, on the
run again, kept his trust in God...

👁 Read verses 24–37

▶ Why did David send the ark back
to Jerusalem? (v25–26)

▶ What did he do when he heard
of Ahithophel's betrayal? (v31)

▶ How did God start to answer
David's prayer? (v32–34)

Now Absalom had to plan his
attack, but he had two advisers —
Ahithophel and now Hushai. Which
would he pick? We'll find out in a
couple days.

THINK IT OVER

David was on the run from his own
son. The situation was bad but he
talked to God about it and sought His
guidance. Do you react like that when
life slaps you in the face?

PRAY ABOUT IT

Talk to God about any tough
situations or big decisions you're
facing. Ask Him to guide you clearly.

➡ TAKE IT FURTHER

A little more on page 124.

79 | From bad to curse

David is God's chosen king. Yet he's been chased out of Jerusalem by his own son, Absalom, who wants David's crown. Today, David meets two more enemies.

👁 **Read 2 Samuel 16 v 1–4**

ENGAGE YOUR BRAIN

ⅅ *What did Ziba have for David and his men? (v1)*

ⅅ *What was Ziba's news about his master, Mephibosheth? (v3)*

ⅅ *What was the good news for Ziba? (v4)*

Good news and bad news. Ziba showed thoughtful kindness to David; but his master, Mephibosheth, (who David had showed great kindness to) had switched sides. But all was not as it seemed. Ziba lied about Meph so he'd be given all Meph's possessions (it's in chapter 19).

THINK IT OVER

ⅅ *Do you ever take advantage of others' hard times?*

ⅅ *Ever lie to gain for yourself?*

👁 **Read verses 5–14**

ⅅ *What did Shimei do? (v5–6)*

ⅅ *What did he claim? (v8)*

ⅅ *What did Abishai want to do?*

ⅅ *What was David's surprising answer? (v11)*

ⅅ *What was David's hope? (v12)*

Amazingly, Shimei got away with cursing, insulting and throwing dirt at the king. But David knew he deserved it for sinning against God. He also knew how gracious and merciful God is. Despite his desperate situation on the run, David knew God could still show him kindness (v12).

PRAY ABOUT IT

God has done that with us. We're all cursed because of our sin. We all deserve death. But God sent His Son to give us eternal life if we trust in Him. Thank God right now.

THE BOTTOM LINE

Hope is never lost with God.

➡ **TAKE IT FURTHER**

The story continues for Ziba and Shimei on page 124.

80 | Hush Hush

The story goes on. Absalom is now hugely popular and aims to kill his father David who has fled to the desert. But David has friends who've infiltrated Absalom's inner circle. Time for Hushai to step up to the mark.

👁 Read 2 Samuel 16 v 15–23

ENGAGE YOUR BRAIN

▷ *How was Hushai clever? (v16–19)*
▷ *What was Ahithophel's nasty advice to Absalom? (v21)*
▷ *Why did Absalom listen to him? (v23)*

👁 Read 2 Samuel 17 v 1–14

▷ *What was Ahithophel's battle plan? (v1–3)*
▷ *How was Hushai's plan different? (v11–13)*
▷ *Why did Absalom surprisingly listen to Hushai? (v14)*

Ahithophel's advice seemed wise — attack immediately and kill only David so the people remain on your side. But Hushai came up with a plan which would buy time for his friend David. Absalom took Hushai's advice because God was working behind the scenes (v14). God often works in quiet, even invisible ways to make His plans work out for His people.

👁 Read verses 15–29

▷ *How would the news get to David? (v15–17)*
▷ *What went wrong? (v18)*
▷ *What went right? (v19–22)*
▷ *What happened to Ahithophel? (v23)*

Things were looking bad for David — on the run with only a small army; his son hunting him down with the backing of most of Judah. But God had other plans and he helped David to escape and prepare properly for the showdown.

PRAY ABOUT IT

How has God been at work in your life, behind the scenes? Thank Him and pray that He will use you to make His perfect plans work out.

THE BOTTOM LINE

God's in control behind the scenes.

→ **TAKE IT FURTHER**

Shhhh... there's more on page 124.

81 | Final showdown

Absalom vs David finally reaches its endgame. The odds are stacked in Absalom's favour. Well, they are if you're relying on soldiers and national popularity. But God holds the key to success and victory.

👁 Read 2 Samuel 18 v 1–8

ENGAGE YOUR BRAIN

▣ *How did David prepare for battle? (v1–2)*

▣ *What did his men think of the plan? (v3)*

▣ *What was David concerned about? (v5)*

▣ *What happened in the forest? (v6–8)*

David's men knew he was God's chosen king and was too valuable to risk in battle, especially as Absalom's army wanted only to kill the king. So David stayed behind and commanded his soliders not to harm his son Absalom. God gave David's army a great victory. But what would happen to Absalom?

👁 Read verses 9–18

▣ *Despite David's orders, what was Joab's intention? (v11)*

▣ *So what happened to handsome, scheming Absalom? (v14–17)*

▣ *What had been Absalom's opinion of himself? (v18)*

Ironic. Absalom, with a handsome face and long flowing hair, gets his head stuck in a tree! David asked for his son to be to be treated gently but Joab was ruthless — Absalom was killed and his body dumped in a pit. Absalom rebelled against God and His chosen king and got what he deserved. The same fate awaits anyone who rejects Jesus and puts themselves first (v18) — they can expect to be punished.

PRAY ABOUT IT

Talk to God about ways you lift yourself up or go against Him, and ask for His help. Pray for a family member who ignores Jesus.

→ TAKE IT FURTHER

No *Take it further* today.

82 Truth hurts

David's men have won a great victory and evil Absalom is dead. How would David take the news?

Read 2 Samuel 18 v 19–33

ENGAGE YOUR BRAIN

- ▣ *Why wouldn't Joab let someone as important as Ahimaaz take the news to David? (v20)*
- ▣ *What did Ahimaaz do?*
- ▣ *But what happened when David asked him about Absalom? (v29)*
- ▣ *What happened w hen David heard the truth? (v33)*

Despite the great victory, Joab knew David would be devastated by his rebellious son's death. So he sent a foreigner with the news. Ahimaaz arrived before this messenger but chickened out of mentioning the bad news. But the Cushite (Ethiopian) got it right — victory for David had to mean death for Absalom (v32). If God's people are to win, then God's enemies must be destroyed. It's a sad truth, but it's a necessary truth.

Read 2 Samuel 19 v 1–8

- ▣ *What effect did David's grief have on the troops? (v2–3)*

- ▣ *What did Joab point out to David? (v5–6)*
- ▣ *What effect would David's attitude have? (v7)*
- ▣ *What did David do? (v8)*

David was a suffering king. His trouble with Absalom was punishment from God for earlier sin (12 v 10–12). He shed tears for his griefs and over his own guilt. Jesus, the perfect King, suffered even more. He cried over *our* griefs and paid the price for *our* sin.

PRAY ABOUT IT

It's time to talk to God and pour out your heart to Him.

→ TAKE IT FURTHER

Focus on Jesus — page 124.

83 | Home sweet home

Do you ever look forward to going home after being away
or after a hard day? And then you get home to chaos
and stress and wish you hadn't bothered? Well, that's
probably how David felt on his way back to Jerusalem.

👁 Read 2 Samuel 19 v 9–15

ENGAGE YOUR BRAIN

- ▶ *What were the people arguing about? (v9–10)*
- ▶ *What did David do to win people back to his side? (v11–13)*
- ▶ *What was the result? (v14–15)*

The people were not sure if they wanted David back as king. He'd done loads for them in the past but then he ran away from Jerusalem. But David won over their hearts and they demanded his return as king. He even forgave traitors like Amasa (17 v 25) to keep everyone happy.

👁 Read verses 16–30

- ▶ *What had Shimei done in the past? (2 Sam 16 v 5–8)*
- ▶ *What was his attitude now? (v18–20)*
- ▶ *What was David's response? (v23)*
- ▶ *What had Ziba claimed about Mephibosheth? (2 Sam 16 v 3–4)*
- ▶ *What did Meph say? (v26–27)*
- ▶ *What did David decide? (v29)*

Again David made wise decisions to unite the people. He forgave horrible Shimei to win over the Benjamites (v17). And he told Mephibosheth and Ziba to divide Saul's land between them, to keep both sides happy. Despite Ziba deceiving him, Meph took it all graciously (v28, 30).

👁 Read verses 31–43

David also showed kindness to loyal old Barzillai. But the people were still bickering among themselves (v41-43).

THINK IT OVER

- ▶ *Do you know any Christians who always argue with each other?*
- ▶ *Is there anyone you often argue or fight with?*
- ▶ *What can you do to make peace and unite Christians?*
- ▶ *How can you show kindness to those who have wronged you?*

Pray about these situations and ask God to help you make things better.

→ TAKE IT FURTHER

No *Take it further* today. Go home.

84 | Horror stories

David's reign as king was never simple. Just as things seemed to be getting back to normal, he faced another rebellion. Warning: this chapter is bloodthirsty and stomach-churningly gory. You've been warned.

👁 **Read 2 Samuel 20 v 1–13**

ENGAGE YOUR BRAIN

▶ What did Sheba claim? (v1)

▶ How did the people of Israel and Judah respond? (v2)

▶ How did Amasa let David down? (v5)

▶ How did Joab take his chance to become commander again? (v8–13)

Sheba was a nasty piece of work and he turned many people against David, God's chosen king. David rightly wanted to wipe him out and stop the rebellion against God and His king. On the way, Joab took the opportunity to brutally murder Amasa, who had replaced him as commander of David's army. Now Joab was in charge again.

👁 **Read verses 14–26**

▶ Where did Joab and his troops trap Sheba? (v15)

▶ How did a wise woman save most of the city? (v18–22)

More gruesome death! But in this one hideous act, a woman saved the entire population of a city that was under attack. Both this woman and Joab make decisions that pay off for them, but result in someone's death.

THINK IT OVER

▶ How have you manipulated situations so you come out best?

▶ When do your morals disappear so you can improve your own situation?

PRAY IT THROUGH

Admit these things to God. Ask His help in putting others first and obeying Him rather than seeking your own advancement at all costs.

➔ **TAKE IT FURTHER**

Another horror story is on page 124.

85 | Human sacrifice

We've been reading loads about the trouble caused by David's own sins. But now David inherits a problem from Saul — it will be an unpleasant one to sort out.

👁 Read 2 Samuel 21 v 1–14

ENGAGE YOUR BRAIN

- ▶ *What was the reason for this terrible famine? (v1)*
- ▶ *What did the Gibeonites demand? (v5–6)*
- ▶ *So what did David do? (v7–9)*
- ▶ *What did Rizpah do? (v10)*
- ▶ *How did David react? (v11–13)*
- ▶ *And what did God do? (v14)*

Three years of famine must have been unbearable. God told David it was because Saul had murdered a load of Gibeonites. To regain God's blessing, David had to please these people. This involved sacrificing human lives. It's horrific, but blood was required to pay for Saul's sin and the breaking of a promise to God. It seems so disgusting because paying for sins *is* horrific. Jesus died a hideous death to pay the price for our sins against God.

👁 Read verses 15–22

- ▶ *What did Ishbi-Benob nearly do to David? (v16)*

- ▶ *What did David's men decide? (v17)*
- ▶ *What happened to Rapha's descendants? (v22)*

The soldiers knew David was God's chosen king, who must be protected at all costs. The giant with twelve fingers and twelve toes must have been terrifying. But when he taunted God's people, he was killed. Ultimately, that's what happens to everyone who stands against God and His people. They will be destroyed. God's people will win in the end.

PRAY ABOUT IT

Thank God that in the end His enemies will be silenced. Thank Him for already winning the victory through Jesus' death in our place.

→ TAKE IT FURTHER

Another sad story on page 125.

86 Powerful God

So far in the story of King David we've seen adultery, murder, family breakdown and war. But David now takes some time out for a song. Yes, really. In his song, David gives us some great truths about God. Listen up.

Read 2 Samuel 22 v 1–4

ENGAGE YOUR BRAIN

- What qualities of God was David shouting about?

Read verses 5–20

- What had been David's situation? (v5–6)
- What did he do about it? (v7)
- What impression of God do we get from v8–16?
- What did God do when David cried for help? (v17–20)

David had been so low and felt so desperate. Many times he thought death was just around the corner. He cried to God for help. The Lord's answer was devastating (v8–16). He was so angry at the way His chosen king was being treated, His fury exploded on David's enemies and they were destroyed. We must never forget what a powerful and terrifying God we worship and how strongly He feels for His people (v20).

Read verses 21–30

- What claim does David make? (v21–25)
- We've seen God's anger against sin, but what is He like to those who live His way? (v26–30)

David isn't saying he's perfect — we know he messed up big time. But in all his ups and downs, he didn't turn away from God. The Lord was still his boss — the one David lived for and served. God loves to rescue those who stick with Him and obey Him.

GET ON WITH IT

- In what ways do you need to obey God more?
- What situations do you need God to rescue you from?
- What do you need to praise and thank God for?
- So what are you waiting for???

→ TAKE IT FURTHER

Keep singing on page 125.

87 ┆ King's chorus ┆

King David's still singing and he doesn't seem to have a sore throat yet. He's so excited about God that he just can't stop the praise bursting out of him.

👁 **Read 2 Samuel 22 v 31–37**

ENGAGE YOUR BRAIN

▷ *What had David's experiences taught him about God? (v31)*
▷ *What had He done for David? (v33–37)*
▷ *What's the answer in v32?*

David was a very powerful man — king of Israel; in charge of God's people. But he kept his feet on the ground. He knew that God gave him all his power and success. God protected David and defeated his enemies. There is only One we can rely on (v32). The Lord is the only God and He cares for His people, protects and guides them through life.

THINK IT OVER

▷ *Do you get proud when you have success in life?*
▷ *How can you give God more glory, recognising all He's done for you?*

👁 **Read verses 38–51**

▷ *Which verses show who was behind David's military success?*
▷ *What did David know about his own success? (v48–51)*
▷ *What was David's response? (v47, 50)*

David looked at life from the right perspective. He'd had some terrible times but he knew that God was always with him and had rescued him from darkness. And David didn't get too big-headed when he enjoyed success. He knew that God was behind the good times. The only correct response to such an awesome God is endless praise and telling everyone about Him.

SHARE IT

▷ *Who can you tell about God helping you through hard times?*
▷ *How can you let people know that God has done so many good things for you?*

➔ **TAKE IT FURTHER**

What about Jesus? Try page 125.

88 | Last words, mighty men

We're nearly at the end of the story of David's reign as king. Today we hear David's last words and meet his mightiest warriors.

👁 Read 2 Samuel 23 v 1–7

▷ How does David describe himself? (v1)

▷ How did God want His king to rule? (v3–4)

▷ What was David confident about? (v5)

▷ What else was he sure about? (v6–7)

👁 Read verses 8–23

▷ Which of these "mighty men" most stands out to you?

▷ Why?

This is a record of David's mightiest and most loyal soldiers. The first three (v8–12) seem to be an elite group who stood their ground when everyone else retreated. God used their courage to give His people victory (v10, 12). Three others risked their lives to fetch water for their king (v13–17). David was so overwhelmed by this that he offered the water as a gift to God, thanking God for them. Abishai and Benaiah were also impressive (v18–23).

These men did incredibly brave feats, but not to make make themselves look great. They were in the service of God and His king, David. They didn't seem to boast of their strength and courage. It was given to them by God so they used it to please Him.

GET ON WITH IT

▷ What abilities and passions has God given you?

▷ How can you use them to serve Him?

▷ How can you use them to help/ serve Christian leaders?

▷ So what exactly are you going to do?

PRAY ABOUT IT

Ask God to give you the strength, courage and ability to serve Him. Pray for His help to do the things you've decided to do.

→ TAKE IT FURTHER

More mighty men (and verses 24–39) on page 125.

89 | The final countdown

We've reached the final chapter of our story
and it's full of as many incidents and surprises
as we'd expect.

👁 Read 2 Samuel 24 v 1–17

▶ *What's the bad news? (v1)*

▶ *What did David command? (v2)*

▶ *Yet how did he feel later? (v10)*

▶ *What horrible decision did David
have to make? (v13)*

▶ *What was his choice? (v14–15)*

▶ *How did God show mercy? (v16)*

We don't know exactly why God
punished His people. It seems that
David's census was sinful. Bible
boffins have various theories. The
answer's not obvious so it can't be
vital to know.

The important facts are that David
sinned, and God rightly punished His
people, but then showed mercy. God
doesn't want to punish people (v16),
but sin must be punished. God is fair
and just and always right.

👁 Read verses 18–25

▶ *What did God require David to
do? (v18, v25)*

▶ *What was God's response? (v25)*

Sin requires a sacrifice before
God stops the punishment. The
punishment for our sin has been
stopped by Jesus sacrificing His own
life for us.

At the end of 2 Samuel there's
no blockbuster finale. But David's
kingdom was still in place — as God
promised him. David was a great king
but entirely human and sinful too. So
2 Samuel also points forward to God's
perfect King, Jesus. One day, His rule
will be fully revealed.

PRAY ABOUT IT

Thank God for what 2 Samuel has
taught you. Think how it has inspired
you to love and obey God more.

→ TAKE IT FURTHER

A tiny bit more on page 125.

90 | Security check

Security. The heavy by the shop door who's practised not smiling. The bodyguard who shadows royalty 24/7. But if we're talking permanent security, here's a song. See just who guards believers and what that protection means.

👁 Read Psalm 91 v 1–8

▷ What can believers say about their relationship with God? (v1–2)

▷ How is God described in these verses?

▷ What is God's protection like? (v4)

Life is scary sometimes. Christians can face all kinds of opposition and temptation. But God is always with His people, protecting them. Instead of trying to cope with life by ourselves, we can find security and protection with God. He is totally faithful and dependable.

👁 Read verses 9–16

▷ What's our responsibility? (v9)

▷ And what will follow? (v10)

▷ What are the great promises for those who love God? v14:

v15:

v16:

This doesn't mean Christians will never have tough times. Obviously many believers are persecuted and some are even killed for their beliefs. But, eternally, we're all safe with God. We will live for ever in a place where there will be no pain or suffering.

The promises in v14–16 are mind-blowing. God will rescue and protect all who love Him and live for Him. He will answer their prayers. He will be with them in times of trouble. He will save them and give them eternal life.

PRAY ABOUT IT

What a psalm! Why not rewrite it in your words, for your own situation? Talk to God about any scary stuff you're facing — ask Him to protect you and give you the courage to let others know you love Him.

→ TAKE IT FURTHER

Snake stomping on page 125.

91 | Rest and reign

Let's be ambitious and tackle two psalms at once.
Psalm 92 is written for the Sabbath — the Old Testament
day of rest. But it's not about lounging around. Psalm 93
is short but packed with powerful truths about God.

👁 **Read Psalm 92 v 1–8**

ENGAGE YOUR BRAIN

🄳 *What should we be singing and shouting about? (v1–3)*

🄳

🄳 *Why? (v4–5)*

🄳

🄳 *How are God's enemies described? (v6–7)*

🄳

🄳 *How is the Lord different? (v8)*

👁 **Read verses 9–15**

🄳 *What's in store for God's enemies? (v9)*

🄳 *How are God's people described? (v12–14)*

🄳 *What keeps them going? (v15)*

👁 **Read Psalm 93 v 1–5**

🄳 *What is God doing and how is He described? (v1)*

🄳 *How long has God reigned and how long will He? (v2)*

The Lord reigns. So what? An awful lot, that's what. The God who chose to reveal Himself to His Old Testament people, Israel — the God of the Bible — is still in charge now. So don't be tempted to think the world's just ticking away by itself. God is reigning from eternity to eternity. He's there and He can't be toppled. Ever.

And since God reigns, we're not in charge. Not you. Not me. A right attitude to God means having a right attitude to ourselves.

PRAY ABOUT IT

Read Psalms 92 and 93 again, telling God what's on your heart as you do so.

→ **TAKE IT FURTHER**

Just a little bit more on page 125.

92 Justice for all

Meet a man in trouble. One who recognises God's in charge of the world. But he looks around and sees injustice — godless people are getting away with stuff. What's going on, God?

👁 Read Psalm 94 v 1–11

▷ What's upsetting the writer? (v3)

▷ What's his prayer? (v1–2)

▷ How do godless people view...

themselves? (v4)

God's people? (v5)

God? (v7)

▷ Why is all of this such a big mistake? (v8–11)

👁 Read verses 12–23

▷ How is v12 different from our natural view of discipline?

▷ How do God's people differ from those who reject Him? (v12–14)

▷ How had God helped this guy? (v17–19)

▷ How do v22–23 answer the question in v20?

THINK IT OVER

▷ How do you respond to God's discipline?

▷ How do you need to alter your view of God after reading this psalm?

PRAY ABOUT IT

Talk to God about...
– the wickedness you see around you.
– people you know who reject God.
– what God's done for you.
– His discipline and judgment.

If you find that hard, use this psalm to help you.

→ TAKE IT FURTHER

No *Take it further* today. Bye!!!

TAKE IT FURTHER

If you want a little more at the end of each day's study, this is where you come. The TAKE IT FURTHER sections give you something extra. They look at some of the issues covered in the day's study, pose deeper questions, and point you to the big picture of the whole Bible.

MATTHEW

The big picture

1 – FAMILY ALBUM

The family tree sums up the history of the people of God in three chunks:

v2–6 tells us of that people growing from one man Abraham to a nation ruled by great King David.

v6–11 traces the collapse of that kingdom, its defeats and its exile to Babylon.

v12–16 follows it after God brought His people back to Jerusalem. They rebuilt the city and waited for God's promised ruler.

ⓘ Which people in v1–17 were good/ bad, rich/poor, Jew/Gentile, male/ female, known/unknown?

A real mixed bunch. Most of them had no idea they were part of God's great plan. We too often have no idea of the real part we have to play in God's plans. We're to get on living for Him, and let Him fit it all together. Sometimes we can look back and see how He's been at work all along.

2 – WHAT'S IN A NAME?

Do you know people who mock the idea of the virgin birth?

ⓘ Do you believe it to be true or not?

ⓘ Why / why not?

ⓘ How might v22–23 help support your firm belief in it?

ⓘ What other things about Jesus showed he wasn't merely human?

ⓘ If Jesus wasn't God, would He be able to save people from their sins? (See 1 Corinthians 5 v 21)

3 – WE TWO KINGS?

The Old Testament quote in v6 is from Micah. **Check out Micah 5 v 2–5.**

ⓘ What do you learn about the identity of this promised ruler? (v2)

ⓘ What will he be like? (v4–5)

ⓘ What will it be like to be one of his people? (v4)

4 – MURDER IN MIND

Does it ever strike you that judgment is a good thing? Herod deserved to be held to account for his atrocious actions and he will be. God is just; He cannot turn a blind eye to evil. When we see or experience injustice, we can long for God to judge and be comforted that He will. The worst crimes that humanity can commit deserve nothing less than hell. And yet Jesus went through that on the cross so we could be forgiven. Justice and mercy. Thank God that He is a God of both.

5 – MAKE WAY FOR THE KING

Read a bit more of Isaiah's prophecy in **Isaiah 40 v 1-11**.

▶ *What does it say about the penalty for Israel's sins? (v2)*

▶ *What do we learn about what God will be like when He comes? (v5, v8, v10-11)*

6 – MAKING A BIG SPLASH

The words *"This is my Son"* are from Psalm 2, which says the Son is the King — God's saying this Jesus is His appointed King. In the past, God called the Israelites "his son"; now it's Jesus who's called that. So Jesus is the true, perfect Son of God. *"Well pleased"*: words from Isaiah 42, where God says His servant will rescue people from sin by suffering and dying.

How does it encourage you to know...
a) Jesus stands with us — so He understands us fully?
b) He stands for us — as our perfect representative to God?
c) He stands in our place — as God's suffering servant?
d) He stands over us — chosen by God to rule for ever?

7 – TEMPTATION SITUATION

Read verses 1–4 again

This is no trivial, sci-fi argument. If Jesus fails to trust God and gives in to the devil, He is sinful like us. In a wrong relationship with God. He'll have His own sin to deal with. So there'd be no rescue, no heaven ahead, no forgiveness.

Jesus is like us, undergoing temptation. Yet He is as we should be: fully trusting God. So He's uniquely qualified. And He chose to complete the task of dealing with our wrong relationship with God — by going to the cross. Thank Him right now.

8 – LIGHT AND LIFE

Without Jesus we are all dead in our sins. Read how **Ephesians 2 v 1–10** describes our natural state and how Jesus has miraculously changed it. Thank Him.

9 – SOMETHING FISHY

Jesus told His first disciples to "fish for people" but just before He returned to heaven he widened that command to all His followers.

Read Matthew 28 v 19–20

▶ *What are we to do?*
▶ *What does Jesus promise us?*

10 – BLESSED IS BEST

Look at all the promises Jesus makes to His followers in verses 3–12. They will be part of His kingdom, they will be comforted, they will inherit the earth, they will be filled with righteousness, they will receive mercy, they will see God, they will be called God's children.

▶ *How does following Jesus, God's King, make all this possible?*

Thank Him now.

11 – COUNT YOUR BLESSINGS

Think a bit more about what it means to be a peacemaker. Check out these passages and then ask God for His help to be a peacemaker.

Romans 5 v 6-11

2 Corinthians 5 v 17–21

Ephesians 2 v 13–15

12 – A SALT COURSE

Notice that Jesus also calls His followers "the light of the world".

Look at John 8 v 12

▶ *Does anything strike you?*

▶ *How are we like Jesus?*

▶ *How is He unique?*

REVELATION
Revealing Jesus

13 – LET'S GET STARTED

First, have a quick flick through the whole book to get a flavour of what Revelation's all about.

Most of it's written in a style called "apocalyptic" — with weird symbol/ number stuff. "Apocalypse" = unveiling. But why's it written like that? Well…

a) it makes for vivid, dramatic teaching. Just soak in the powerful overall effect;

b) it's describing the unseen spiritual world, which can't be easily described using normal language;

c) it uses images and pictures from the Old Testament;

d) it was a familiar style for John's first readers.

Much of Revelation describes world events (not precisely, but giving the big picture). And it does so using several series of sevens, each symbolising different things:

Chapters 6–7: seven seals, symbolising cruel rulers;

Chapters 8–11: seven trumpets, symbolising chaos;

Chapters 12–14: seven signs, symbolising persecution;

Chapters 15–16: seven plagues, symbolising destruction.

Each series of seven describes the same period of history — the time between Jesus' resurrection and His return — but from a different angle. Don't place them one after the other, like one long story. And it's not designed to help us identify specific wars, famines or the day your dog was sick on your doorstep. Don't treat it like a horoscope; remember that Revelation is God revealing to us the truth about Jesus and His plans for us.

14 – SON SHINING

Read verse 9 again

This theme (Christians sticking with Jesus and hanging in there) appears loads in Revelation. Are you living with God in charge as part of His kingdom? Great! >>

And sharing in suffering because of Jesus, and keeping going? Greater!

Read verse 18

Jesus holding the keys to death and Hades (hell) shows His victory over death and sin and the devil. He achieved this through His death and resurrection. Many people think that we're heading towards a massive cosmic battle at the end of the world. But through His death and resurrection, Jesus has already defeated death. His absolute control over death and Hades is great news for John, for the churches and for us. He has ultimate control over death, the last enemy.

Read verse 20

There are various opinions about what's meant by the "angel" of each church. Some people think it means the church leader or maybe the person who first took the letter to each church. We think it probably means an actual angel, a spiritual being. This reminds us that the life of each earthly church is intimately connected with heavenly, spiritual stuff.

15 – CHURCH NEWS LETTER

There's a pattern to each of the letters to the seven churches:

1. A description of Jesus
2. He praises what's good (except Sardis and Laodecia)
3. He criticises what's wrong (except Smyrna and Philadephia)
4. He gives instructions
5. He gives a promise for those who

"overcome"

Now find the pattern in each letter.

16 – GOOD NEWS, BAD NEWS

Read verses 15–17 again

The churches in both Ephesus and Pergamum had to deal with the false teaching of the Nicolaitans. We don't know much about them, but they were clearly leading people away from God with their wrong teaching.

And what's all this about hidden manna and a white stone (v17)? The hidden manna is probably talking about the great stuff God will give His people in eternal life. The white stone may have been used as a ticket to gain entry to gladiator events. Every believer will have a "stone" with his or her name on it, guaranteeing access to the presence of God.

Read verse 28

Many clever people have many different ideas about the promise of the morning star. One of them is linked to Balaam, whose false teaching had crept into the churches of Pergamum and Thyatira. Despite being a sorceror and a false prophet in the Old Testament, Balaam did speak of a "star" that would rise from God's people and rule the nations (Numbers 24 v 17). Jesus is that morning star (Revelation 22 v 16), and He will be the gift to those who remain faithful to Him.

17 – POKING AND PERKING

Read verse 8 again

What's the "open door" that Jesus has set before us and how can we get through it?

▷ *What help does Luke 13 v 22–30 give?*

▷ *How has this door been opened? (Hebrews 10 v 19–22)*

18 – LUKEWARM LAODICEA

Read verse 16

▷ *Have you gone lukewarm in your love for Jesus and the gospel?*

▷ *Why? What is it that has taken your eyes off Him?*

▷ *Will you accept Jesus' verdict on you? (v17–18)*

▷ *Will you respond to His correction? (v19–20)*

Think back over all the seven letters. Here's the early church in all its strengths, enthusiasm and disaster areas.

▷ *How is the church nowadays still like that?*

▷ *What action needs to be taken in your church and your own life?*

19 – HEAVENLY VIEW

Read verses 3–6 again

Precious stones (jasper, carnelian, emerald) remind us of God's covenant agreement with Israel — Exodus 28 v 17–21;
The rainbow reminds us of God's covenant with creation — Genesis 9 v 12–16;
Lightning etc points to God's covenant and laws at Sinai — Exodus 20 v 18;
The sea of glass reminds us of the covenant confirmed — Exodus 24 v 9–10.

20 – LION OR LAMB?

**Read Ezekiel 2 v 9–10
then Zechariah 5 v 1–3,
and then Daniel 12 v 4 & 9**

The scroll could also stand for the problem of human sin in the presence of God. Only Jesus could deal with that. What's *in* the scroll? Wait for chapter 6 — words of judgment on sin, to be revealed before Jesus returns.

**Read Revelation 5 v 6
and check out John 1 v 29
and 1 Corinthians 5 v 7**

▷ *Why is Jesus described as a lamb?*

▷ *What did His death achieve?*

▷ *How does it fulfill what was going on in the Old Testament?*

21 – DARK RIDERS

**Re-read verses 1–8
and then Mark 13 v 5–8**

Jesus is saying: Don't be deceived or alarmed. These things have to happen, but don't mean the end is imminent. Revelation is not concerned with only the final end times, but all of history and Jesus' role in it.

22 – MAKING A STAND

The events of chapter 7 v 1–8 are a flashback. They can't take place after the events of chapter 6. God's people are marked in advance so they'll be secure on God's Day of Judgment. Great news!

The answer to the question posed in Revelation 6 v 17 is that these people are the ones who can stand *"before the throne and before the Lamb"* with the white robes and palm branches of victory. And they can do this, not because of their own righteousness, but because *"salvation belongs to our God... and to the Lamb"*.

23 – INCENSED AND FIERY

On ecological disasters and the end of the world, John Richardson writes: "The opening of the first four seals and trumpets brings about a sequence of what we today would describe as 'ecological disasters'." So, do current ecological disasters indicate that the end of the world is imminent?

In the past, earthquakes, famines and disease could only be linked indirectly to the fall of mankind. Today, deforestation, the extinction of animal species, global warming etc are more obviously linked to our impact on the environment. In this sense, these disasters can be seen more clearly to be a consequence of human sin, and therefore to be warnings of judgment to come.

However, there is no way of knowing whether Christ's return is just around the corner or centuries in the future. Ecological disasters tell us we're heading towards the Second Coming, but they don't tell us how far down the road we still have to travel. The thing to remember is that Christians should be encouraged rather than frightened by this knowledge. **Check out Luke 21 v 26–28.**

24 – SCORPION ATTACK

Read verses 3–11 again and then Joel 1 v 4–6 and 2 v 4, 31
Some Bible experts have claimed the locusts/scorpions are tanks and weapons. But they'd be strange weapons that didn't kill people! Joel shows us that we should see these horrifying creatures as the demonic forces that lie behind mankind's suffering.

26 – EXPERT WITNESS

Let's clear up some of the confusing stuff.
v2: What happens to the many who are in the outer court of the temple, but are not worshippers around the altar?

🔹 *What lessons are there here for any who like religion but don't trust Jesus?*

v4: See Zechariah 4 v 1–6. The olive trees and lampstands represent Christians and the church.

v7–12: There will be a time before Jesus returns when the gospel witness of the church will be suppressed. This seems to be the same as the "time of the anti-Christ", which we'll read more about in chapters 17 and 20.

v19: In the Old Testament, the ark of the covenant was a wooden box that symbolised the throne or presence of God with His people. In the New Testament it symbolises God's faithfulness in keeping His covenant agreement with His people.

27 – CITY CENTRE

Read Zechariah 8 v 20–23

This is a glimpse of a perfect future with God. People will be drawn to Him from all over the world. That's already happening isn't it? And one day, thanks to Jesus, God will again live with His chosen people.

2 SAMUEL
Kingdom come

28 – A SAD START

Welcome to fast-paced 2 Samuel. Here's how it fits together:

Chapters 1–4:   David's rise to power in Judah

Chapters 5–10:   His rule as king over all Israel

Chapters 11–12: David's personal crisis

Chapters 13–20: Its results: like father, like sons

Chapters 21–24: Final incidents, summaries, songs

29 – TRIBAL TROUBLE

Read 2 Samuel 3 v 2–5

This may seem like a dull list of wives and babies but some of these names will play a big part in the unfolding story. Amnon did some really bad stuff (chapter 13), Absalom tried to overthrow his father and become king (chapters 13–19), and Adonijah did the same (1 Kings 1–2).

31 – KING AT LAST

Read 2 Samuel 5 v 2
then John 10 v 11–18
and 1 Peter 2 v 25

▶ *What makes Jesus such a great*
shepherd?

▶ *How should you respond to Him?*

32 – CONQUERING KING

Read verses 13–16

David acquired more wives and concubines (mistresses) and loads more children. On the one hand, the number of David's sons indicates his strength. On the other hand, the number of wives and mistresses reveals his sin and foolishness. Having many wives and concubines was going against God's rules for his king (Deuteronomy 17 v 17). David was a great king, but he was flawed. Jesus is the only true king who always does what pleases His Father.

Read verse 20

"Baal Perazim" means "Lord of burstings out", to remind the Israelites of the way God had broken down the Philistines, as a massive flood of water smashes everything in its path. That's our all-powerful God.

33 – FEAR AND LOATHING IN JERUSALEM

Read verses 3–7 again
and then Numbers 4 v 4–6, 15, 17–20

▶ *How did the people break God's rules*
for His ark?

The Lord had given specific instructions about how the ark should be transported: no touching, no looking, no carting. Everything was to be covered and then the Kohathites were not to look upon any of it so they didn't die. God gave these rules so that people didn't die. He didn't want anyone to die. David and Uzzah had

115

plenty of warning. Uzzah acted foolishly because he forgot who he was dealing with. Often, God's people forget the holiness of the God they face. We don't need to be terrified of our loving Creator, but a bit more fear would be healthy!

34 – HOME SWEET HOME
Re-read verses 5–16
Chapter 7 is a highlight in 1 & 2 Samuel. In fact, God's covenant here is a huge Old Testament moment. It follows God's covenant with Noah, Abraham and Moses. Now the covenant agreement is with David, who receives far more from God than he could ever have hoped. It's an act of God that shows His great, ongoing commitment to His people.
▶ *What does this covenant show us God is like?*

35 – PRAYERS AND PROMISES
David didn't sulk when God turned down his request to build a temple.
▶ *Which parts of David's prayer show His obedience to God?*
▶ *Do you submit to God as your King or do you insist on being boss?*

36 – WINNING WAYS
Read verses 15–18
▶ *How is David's reign (so far) summed up? (v15)*
▶ *Who helped him? (v16–18)*

On the whole, David was doing what a God-fearing king should. He wasn't perfect, but he did serve God. Likewise,

we mess up sometimes, but we can still serve God wherever He has placed us — at school, in a mind-numbing job, in a difficult family situation. If we live with God as King, being part of His kingdom, people will eventually take notice.

It's also good, like David, to have back-up. He appointed all kinds of people in His kingdom (v16–18). We can ask other Christians to pray for us and study the Bible with us. We need to use all the back-up we can get!

38 – THE CHEEK OF IT!
Read verses 10–12 again
Joab is a mixed character throughout the book. Sometimes vicious and cruel, sometimes showing faith in God.
▶ *How does his faith in God shine through in these verses?*
▶ *Do you lean on God as he did?*
▶ *How can you show your faith in God more in the way you act?*

39 – HOME ALONE
**Read 2 Samuel 9 v 1–3
then 2 Samuel 10 v 1–2
and then 2 Samuel 11 v 1–5**
▶ *How does David act differently in these stories?*

In the first two situations David was eager to show kindness to both Israelites and Ammonites. But in chapter 11 David has no kindness to show. This is God's chosen king and he's behaving disgustingly. Never think you're beyond falling like this. If King

David can do such terrible things, then any of us can. Stay on your guard and ask God to help you fight temptation.

40 – TWIST IN THE TALE
Read 2 Samuel 12 v 26–31

▷ *While David was having his crisis, what was Joab doing? (v26)*

▷ *What did he do for his king and why? (v28)*

▷ *Despite David's sin, what did God do for him? (v29–31)*

David's victory was a sign that God had forgiven him. Of course it's wrong for us to sin. Equally, it's wrong for us to live in the past after we've confessed those sins.

MATTHEW

41 – THE BIG PICTURE

It can be quite helpful to imagine the history of God's people like a huge hourglass. The number of true believers in Israel gets smaller and smaller until it reaches Jesus at the centre of the timer. He is the only faithful descendant of Abraham. But as God's new people, the church, grows, the hourglass gets bigger again because we have all passed through the centre — we are all "in Christ" as the Bible puts it.

42 – KILLER INSTINCT

Quick action to heal grievances can easily be put off by excuses like: *"It's gone too far already"*, *"We're just different personalities"*, *"I'll lose too much face"*,

or *"I don't care"*.

▷ *Instead, how will you make speedy reconciliation a habit?*

43 – SERIOUS SEX STUFF
Read verses 29–30 again

If the first look ("your eye") sends your mind into fantasies, Jesus says "Don't look". If what you do ("your hand") is a source of sexual temptation, don't put yourself in those situations. Jot down what changes this will mean practically for you.

▷ *Are you prepared to take the ridicule such action might bring?*

Read verses 31–32

Jesus quotes the Jewish leaders' (wrong) teaching of an OT command. Some rabbis were making divorce easy (eg: if your wife burns your food or doesn't look nice, kick her out), but Jesus wanted to teach that marriage was permanent.

▷ *What does Jesus say is the only reason for divorce?*

▷ *What is ending a marriage for any other reason seen as?*

44 – YES = YES? EYE = EYE?
Read verses 38–42 again and then Romans 12 v 19–21

Who drives you mad, irritates you or laughs at you? Those who persecute you are the hardest to love. Now write down on paper what you can say or do to show them love. And when you'll do it.

▷ *What will you pray for them?*

▷ *You can't pray for someone without loving them, right?*

117

45 – LOVE YOUR ENEMY

The rabbis (v43) had twisted the Old Testament command (*"love your neighbour"*) by leaving out the *"as yourself"* bit and adding *"hate your enemy"*. No way, says Jesus.

▶ *What two things are Christians to do to their enemies? (v44)*

▶ *Why must we? (v45)*

God's care is indiscriminate — it includes everyone. So if you're only good to your mates, big deal.

▶ *So what do you need to change and how exactly will you do it?*

46 – GODLY GIVING

Pretending to be holy, we can fool others and we can even fool ourselves, but we can't fool God. Take a look ahead to **Matthew 7 v 21–24.**

▶ *What is the warning?*

▶ *What must we do? (v24)*

See also **James 1 v 22–27.**

47 – HOW TO PRAY

▶ *What sort of God do you pray to?*

He's not like a slot machine to fire requests at, or a computer just to babble at mechanically, or a genie who meets our every wish. He's the one true God. And He's our loving, heavenly Father. Don't, like the Pharisees, pray selfishly and mindlessly. Put God's concerns first, but also tell Him your needs. The Lord's Prayer says He meets all human needs: physical (food etc), spiritual (forgiveness) and moral (strength to live His way).

48 – BANKING ON GOD

Look again at verses 21–23

Here's a test: What do you daydream about most?

That is where your heart is. Ask God to change your heart if that needs to happen. Check out **Ezekiel 36 v 25–27.**

49 – WHY WORRY?

Memorising Scripture is a good antidote to worry — it makes us think of God's kingdom (v33) and it reminds us of the character of the King we serve. Why not try learning **Psalm 23** and **Romans 8 v 38–39** for starters?

50 – PLANK YOU VERY MUCH

▶ *In what situations are you most tempted to be judgmental?*

▶ *Who do you criticise the most?*

▶ *Is there a Bible verse that can help you in that situation?*

Pray about the issue and ask God to change your heart.

51 – KNOCK-ON EFFECT

Have you ever sung the old hymn *Before the Throne of God Above*? The lyrics are a great reminder of why we can have confidence in prayer. Use them now as you talk to God.

Before the throne of God above
I have a strong, a perfect plea:
a great High Priest, whose name is Love,
who ever lives and pleads for me.
My name is graven on his hands,
my name is written on his heart;

I know that while in heaven he stands
no tongue can bid me to depart.

When Satan tempts me to despair,
and tells me of the guilt within,
upward I look, and see him there
who made an end of all my sin.
Because the sinless Saviour died,
my sinful soul is counted free;
for God, the Just, is satisfied
to look on him and pardon me.

Behold him there, the risen Lamb!
My perfect, spotless Righteousness,
the great unchangeable I AM,
the King of glory and of grace!
One with himself, I cannot die;
my soul is purchased by his blood;
my life is hid with Christ on high,
with Christ, my Saviour and my God.
(Charitie Lees Bancroft)

52 – HIT THE ROAD

Have you ever tried using a simple gospel outline to help you explain what it means to follow Jesus? Two Roads (available from The Good Book Company) is one version that's easy to learn, or give to a friend.

53 – BAD TASTE

This section of Matthew 7 v 15–27 is all about putting our money where our mouth is, having a living faith rather than merely paying lip-service to Jesus.

🄳 *Can you see the connection between verses 20, 21 and 24?*

54 – LORD! LORD!

It can be easy to misread the Sermon on the Mount as a list of impossible standards to try and live up to. But remember how it starts, with Jesus talking to those who are already His. The way into His kingdom is by acknowledging our spiritual poverty and sin, and casting ourselves on His mercy. Once we are His, He will change us by His Spirit so that the picture painted in chapters 5–7 becomes truer and truer of our lives.

55 – FIRM FOUNDATIONS
Read James 1 v 22–25

🄳 *How can you remember to do this?*
Think about what you read in the Bible; come back to it during the day. Perhaps get a Christian friend to ask you how you are doing at listening and putting Jesus' words into practice. Check out **Hebrews 10 v 23–25** to see why it is so helpful for Christians to meet together regularly to do this.

PSALMS

56 – DOWN IN THE PIT
Read 1 Corinthians 13 v 8–12

🄳 *What won't last for ever? (v8)*
🄳 *What will never fail?*
However bad things seem, we can trust in God's unfailing love.

🄳 *How will eternal life compare to our current imperfect life? (v12)*
🄳 *How can v12 encourage you during dark times?*

57 – SHOUT IT OUT!
Read verses 1–2 again

▶ *How exactly will you sing or shout about God's love?*

▶ *How can you share His faithfulness with those around you?*

▶ *What about to people of a different generation to you?*

REVELATION

59 – REVEALING JESUS
Read verse 11 again

▶ *Are we willing to lay down our lives for Christ, if that's necessary?*

▶ *If not, what would hold us back?*

Victory in "spiritual warfare" isn't achieved by special people or special methods. Satan is overcome by the gospel in the life of ordinary Christians. So hang in there, relying on Jesus' death and living to obey God.

60 – SIMPLY THE BEAST
Read verse 18

John Richardson writes: *"Probably more has been preached and written on the number of the beast than any other passage of scripture with over 100 different interpretations of 666."* People try to use the number to calculate a name, but they're missing the point. In Revelation, John tells his audience to calculate the number, not the name. He tells us it's a human number, 666.

The number six is seen as representing humans. Seven is the perfect number in Revelation and three often stands for God (the trinity). So 777 would be a good number to represent God. *"666 is then the number of man pretending to be God. A man whose personality and word dominates society in a godlike way. Hitler, Mao, Stalin, Hussein and others have all been mentioned. No doubt the final antichrist will have the same characteristics and 666 will describe him well."*

61 – ANGELIC MESSAGES
Read verse 4 again

This isn't saying they were virgins for life, but that they were concerned for sexual purity. They also *"follow the Lamb wherever he goes"*. And where did Jesus go? To His death. See **Mark 8 v 34** and ask God to help your commitment to Jesus be greater than your fear of death.

Read verse 13

People who have died remaining faithful to Jesus will be blessed. And when they die they finally get to rest and be at peace. And get this: *"their deeds will follow them"*. Paul Barnett says this: *"That they have regarded Christ as more important than death cannot fail to make a positive impact on those who observe their commitment ... If they back up their gospel [message] with willingness to die for Jesus as their true leader, then perhaps His claims to be ruler should be investigated.*

Read Matthew 13 v 24–30 & 36–43

▶ *How would you summarise what Jesus is saying here?*

▶ *What's the bad news?*

▶ *What's the good news?*

▶ *What does it make you want to say to God right now?*

Read Revelation 16 v 13–16
More helpful stuff from John Richardson: *"As the end nears, so the enemies of God become more frantic in their opposition to Him. In the final phase of demonic deception, the human kingdoms are gathered against God by repulsive spirits which go out from the mouths of the unholy trinity of Satan, the beast and the false prophet (v13).*

But it is all by God's will, since the battle that follows is described as being 'on the great day of God the almighty' (v14) and the words of encouragement in the hour of darkness (v15) are clearly those of Jesus Himself (see Matthew 24 v 43–44). The response of Christians to all these events must be to stay awake and alert, neither giving up nor becoming complacent in the face of what is happening in the world."

Verse 16 — remember that this is a vision, so don't expect a huge final battle of Armageddon with actual armies. This is a spiritual battle, and Jesus has already won!

Read verses 9–14
Here the angel reveals things for a *"mind with wisdom"* — no wonder it's so hard to understand! The seven heads, hills and kings here (v10) probably symbolise the principle of absolute power and rule (kings and regimes) that claims to be more powerful than God.

Bible experts often interpret *"five have fallen, one is, the other is yet to come"* as referring to specific kings in history but it's hard to know exactly which ones to include and which to leave out. What is definitely true is that many powers have fallen and we live under a "power" now, and there will be one more to come *"for a little while"*. This may be referring to the time of the Antichrist.

The beast (v11) is identified with the corrupt rulers of this world. There are also a further ten horns/kings to come (v12). Ten is a symbol of magnitude (a huge number of something) and horns are a symbol of power. So it seems that a great human power will have great influence at the same time as the beast (v13). But this will only last a short time (v12) and Jesus, the *"Lord of lords and King of kings"*, will defeat them! (v14)

Babylon features throughout the Bible in different ways.
a) Babel — a spiritual rebellion against God (Genesis 11 v 1–9);
b) The Babylonian empire — the historical

121

enemy of God's people (see Psalm 137, Isaiah chapters 13, 14, 47);

c) Babylon representing the godless society (here in Revelation).

The Babylonian empire (b) was used by God to bring punishment against His own people. Do you see how God's doing that with godless society today?

66 – WHITE WEDDING

For more on God's people being Christ's bride, check out **Isaiah 54 v 5, Jeremiah 31 v 32, and Ephesians 5 v 25–32.**

Read Revelation 19 v 10 again

"The testimony of Jesus is the spirit of prophecy" — speaking about Jesus brings God's word to people. Sharing the gospel with people is more powerful than you might think. Try it!

67 – CONQUERING KING

Read verses 19–21 again

The enemies of God gather at Armageddon, but the battle's over before it's begun (v20). When Jesus finally comes, there's no battle to be fought, only a word to be spoken. Jesus wins — because He's won already.

68 – SATAN'S DOOM

Here are the three different views of the 1000 years:

Premillennialism – Christ returns before (pre) the 1000 years

Christ returns with His saints, destroying the beast, the false prophet and all their armies. Satan is removed from the earth and "bound" in the pit. Christians are resurrected to rule over the earth with Jesus. After 1000 years (the millennium), Satan is allowed out of this pit and leads a rebellion against this rule. At the last moment, God intervenes, burns up the rebellious armies and throws Satan into the fiery lake. All the dead are then resurrected for the final judgment. A new heaven and earth are established.

Postmillennialism – Christ returns after (post) the 1000 years

The church overcomes the powers of satanically manipulated politics and false ideology (the beast and the false prophet) in the present age. Metaphorically, they are thrown into the lake of fire. There follows a period of peace and prosperity (the millennium) when Satan is "bound". His influence pretty much disappears and the church can be said to rule the world. However, Satan's power is allowed to re-emerge for one great rebellion against God — the period of the Antichrist. This rebellion is defeated and Satan is thrown into the fiery lake as Christ returns to judge the world. A new heaven and earth are established.

Amillennialism – the 1000 years are a metaphor for the present age

In the present, the beast and the false prophet (satanically manipulated politics and false ideology) oppress and oppose the church, but Satan himself is "bound" during this time ("1000 years" but it could be much longer). His powers are restricted and the nations are able to hear the gospel. From a heavenly point of view, Christians already live and reign with Christ. However, in the very last days Satan's power is released again and a period of deception and suffering follows, including massive persecution of Christians — the period of the Antichrist. When Christ rules with the saints, He destroys these powers and all those who've followed them. Satan too. After this, the dead are raised and judged — unbelievers go their punishment and believers go to eternal life. A new heaven and earth are established.

69 – THE FUTURE'S BRIGHT
Read Isaiah 65 v 17–25

▷ *When Jesus returns, what will change? (v17)*
▷ *What will this new city be like? (v18–19)*
▷ *How else will it be great?*
   v21–22:
   v23:
   v24:
   v25:

Mind-blowing stuff. This whole sinful world will be replaced with a new creation. Nothing harmful will be a part of it (v25) and believers will live in this paradise with God.

70 – BRIGHT LIGHTS, BIG CITY
The first chapter of the Bible shows how God made the world. The last chapter shows how He will remake it.

A few things to clear up...

21 v 15–17: Don't take this literally — by this reckoning, God's new world is a cube with each side as long as the distance from London to Athens. It's probably better to view it as a picture of a perfect, glorious, immense, cosmic new creation of God.

21 v 22: In the Old Testament, the temple is the symbol of God's presence with His people. In God's new world, there's no need for pictures: God and the Lamb (Jesus) will be there in person.

22 v 1–2: The river idea flows from **Ezekiel 47 v 1–12**.

71 – THE LAST WORD
Read verse 9

"Worship God, not the beast" has been the challenge in Revelation. Everyone who reads Revelation must choose between two possible objects of worship, belong to one of two communities, and face one of two destinies.

OBADIAH

Tables turned

72 – PRIDE BEFORE A FALL
Read Genesis 25 v 21–26

Jacob and Esau even fought in the womb! Jacob's descendants were God's people and Esau's were the Edomites. No wonder the two nations were always fighting. Esau sold his rights as elder son (Genesis 25) and so opted out of God's special care.

>>>>

Read Hebrews 12 v 15–17

Esau's choice set his destiny: he showed no repentance, just self pity (v17). For the right response to God, **read v18–29.**

73 – RELATIVE TROUBLE

Back pedal to Matthew 5 v 10–12

▶ *Why should Christians "rejoice and be glad"?*

▶ *To whom does the kingdom of heaven belong?*

▶ *How does this encourage you to keep going when it's hard?*

Think of some reasons why the gospel offends people.

74 – MOUNTAIN RESCUE

Read Isaiah 63 v 1–6

Edom is used as a picture of the world's hostility to God. Its destruction is a picture of the Messiah's conquest of sin and His great rescue — all fulfilled by Jesus.

▶ *Is it possible to accept Jesus' rescue but not let Him be King of your life?*

▶ *So how should that affect life as a Christian?*

2 SAMUEL

76 – KINGDOM COME

The focus for chapters 13–19 is Absalom, David's third son (2 Sam 3 v 2–5). Amnon was the firstborn, Absalom the third. We presume number 2 in line to the throne, Kileab, died in childhood as he's never mentioned again.

▶ *What examples in chapter 13 do you want to avoid? Why?*

78 – SON RISE

Read verses 25–26 again

This wasn't David giving up on God. Oh no. This showed he wasn't superstitious about the ark — as if it was a magic charm to keep God on his side. Instead, David's attitude was: *"Let God do to me whatever seems good to Him".*

▶ *Could you say this to Him?*

▶ *How does David's reliance on God encourage you?*

79 – FROM BAD TO CURSE

For more on both Shimei and Ziba, check out **2 Samuel 19 v 18–30.**

80 – HUSH HUSH

Read 2 Samuel 17 v 23

Ahithophel was not just a top adviser who switched sides and made a mistake. He turned against God's chosen king, David, so he was an enemy of God. And now he's dead. His death is a sign of what will happen to all the enemies of God's true King. You can't attack God's people and God's King without eventually being crushed by the power God. The Lord protects His people and punishes sin.

82 – TRUTH HURTS

Read Isaiah 53 v 1–12

Read this slowly, verse by verse. Think how it accurately describes Jesus. Turn your thoughts into prayers of thanks.

84 – HORROR STORIES

Read verse 3 again, then 2 Samuel 12 v 9–12,

and then 2 Samuel 16 v 20–22

God had told David this would happen as part of David's punishment for adultery and murder. Absalom slept with David's concubines to disgrace David. Sad. It's especially sad when people's lives are ruined by the sin of others.

85 – HUMAN SACRIFICE

Read verses 10–14 again

What a sad story! But sometimes it's totally appropriate to be sad, to mourn, and to remember people we miss and sad stuff that's happened. We often try to stay cheerful, but sometimes we need to let these feelings flow over us, whether we're alone, pouring it out to a friend or sharing it with the Lord.

86 – POWERFUL GOD

David's song is also in the Bible as Psalm 18. It gives us an amazing picture of God. David faced death, but the Lord answered his prayers and rescued him. This terrifying, all-powerful God stepped in and showed great love and care for David. No wonder David's singing His praises.

🄳 How have you seen God's power?
🄳 How have you seen His care?

87 – KING'S CHORUS

**Read verse 36 again
then Philippians 2 v 5–11
and 2 Corinthians 8 v 9**

🄳 How did Jesus stoop down to make us great?
🄳 What's incredible about what Jesus did?

88 – LAST WORDS, MIGHTY MEN

Read verses 24–39

This isn't just a list of names. These men were all outstanding soldiers, defending God's kingdom. God used them to protect His people and so they're namechecked here. The Bible is full of lists. It seems that God never tires of naming His faithful people. And did you notice the last name in the list? A reminder that David (and his men) were not perfect. But God, in His grace, uses even sinful people like us in His perfect plans.

89 – THE FINAL COUNTDOWN

Read verses 16–18 again

Exciting — it was here that God's temple would later be built by Solomon (2 Chronicles 3 v 1). God was working out the promises He'd made to David back in chapter 7.

90 – SECURITY CHECK

Read verses 11–13

The devil tried to use these verses against Jesus (Luke 4 v 9–13). For us, v11–12 means we'll look back and see God's hand on our lives, protecting us. So, can we tread on lions and snakes (v13)? Well, it's more likely the lion represents strong opposition and the snake is subtle oppo.

91 – REST AND REIGN

Read Psalm 92 v 4–5

On spare paper, list some of the works of God that are great... and some of the truths about Him that blow you away.

engage wants to hear from YOU!

▶ Share experiences of God at work in your life
▶ Any questions you have about the Bible or the Christian life?
▶ How can we make *engage* better?

Email us — **martin@thegoodbook.co.uk**

Or send us a letter/postcard/cartoon/treasure chest to:

engage 37 Elm Road, New Malden, Surrey, KT3 3HB, UK

In the next **engage**

1 Corinthians God, the bad and the ugly

1 Kings Ruling passion

Song of Solomon Love song

Matthew True faith

Plus: Prayer

Homosexuality

The Christian crutch

Toolbox & Real Lives

Order **engage** now!

Make sure you order the next issue of **engage**. Or even better, grab a one-year subscription to make sure **engage** lands in your hands as soon as it's out.

Call us to order in the UK on 0333 123 0880

International: +44 (0) 20 8942 0880

or visit your friendly neighbourhood website:

UK: www.thegoodbook.co.uk

N America: www.thegoodbook.com

Australia: www.thegoodbook.com.au

New Zealand: www.thegoodbook.co.nz

Growing with God

Faithful, contemporary Bible reading resources for every age and stage.

NEW!

Beginning with God
For pre-schoolers

Table Talk & XTB
Table Talk for 4-11s and their parents, *XTB* for 7-11s

Discover
For 11-13s

Engage
For 14-18s

Explore
For adults

All Good Book Company Bible reading resources...

- ❯ have a strong focus on practical application
- ❯ encourage people to read the Bible for themselves
- ❯ explain Bible passages in context
- ❯ cover Bible books in the Old and New Testament

UK: www.thegoodbook.co.uk
N America: www.thegoodbook.com
Australia: www.thegoodbook.com.au
New Zealand: www.thegoodbook.co.nz

the good book
COMPANY